Terrie Cousins-Brown

The Complete
Polish Lowland Sheepdog

© Copyright 2005 Terrie Cousins-Brown.

All rights reserved. No part of this publication may be reproduced, stored in a retrieval system, or transmitted, in any form or by any means, electronic, mechanical, photocopying, recording, or otherwise, without the written prior permission of the author.

Note for Librarians: a cataloguing record for this book that includes Dewey Decimal Classification and US Library of Congress numbers is available from the Library and Archives of Canada. The complete cataloguing record can be obtained from their online database at:
www.collectionscanada.ca/amicus/index-e.html
ISBN 1-4120-4525-8

Printed in Victoria, BC, Canada

 *Printed on paper with minimum 30% recycled fibre. Trafford's print shop runs on "green energy" from solar, wind and other environmentally-friendly power sources.*

TRAFFORD

Offices in Canada, USA, Ireland and UK

This book was published *on-demand* in cooperation with Trafford Publishing. On-demand publishing is a unique process and service of making a book available for retail sale to the public taking advantage of on-demand manufacturing and Internet marketing. On-demand publishing includes promotions, retail sales, manufacturing, order fulfilment, accounting and collecting royalties on behalf of the author.

Book sales for North America and international:
Trafford Publishing, 6E–2333 Government St.,
Victoria, BC v8t 4p4 CANADA
phone 250 383 6864 (toll-free 1 888 232 4444)
fax 250 383 6804; email to orders@trafford.com

Book sales in Europe:
Trafford Publishing (UK) Ltd., Enterprise House, Wistaston Road Business Centre,
Wistaston Road, Crewe, Cheshire cw2 7rp UNITED KINGDOM
phone 01270 251 396 (local rate 0845 230 9601)
facsimile 01270 254 983; orders.uk@trafford.com

Order online at:
trafford.com/04-2333

10   9   8   7   6   5   4   3   2

Acknowledgements

Dr Tomasz Borkowski and **Dr Malgorzata Supronowicz** - for continually inspiring and supporting me.

The Breed Standard Committee - **Dr Tomasz Borkowski, Dr Anna Dominiak, Barbara Larska, Andrzej Stepinski** - for use of the proposed Standard Commentary.

Beata Lesniak-Malecka - for allowing me to use many black and white photographs from her personal collection; these photographs were taken by **Dr Danuta Hryniewicz**.

Barbara Larska - for sending photos from her archive collection and allowing me to use images from her book *Ksiega Championow 2000*.

Katja Jasica - for use of her drawings and photographs.

Karen Robinson, Ula Staszczyk, Dr Anna Dominiak, Wanda Sooby - for additional information, proof reading, editing and translation.

All my friends in Poland - for help, advice and allowing use of their photographs, too numerous to mention individually.

My husband **Ian** for all his encouragement, support and patience.

Cover Picture: Ch.Int.Ch Antrosu Dobrany from Dorianblue ('Dusan'). Owned by the author; bred by Sue Ainsley.

The Complete Polish Lowland Sheepdog

Contents

Acknowledgements	2
Introduction	5
1. The History of the Breed	7
2. The Early Pioneers	19
3. The Breed Standard	34
4. Judging the Polish Lowland Sheepdog	60
5. Breeding and Choosing Your Puppy	74
6. Living with PONs	86
7. Caring for Your PON	91
8. Grooming and Coat Care	97
9. PONs of Influence	102
10. Looking to the Future	112
References	114

This book is dedicated to my mother, Barbara, who gave me my interest in dogs and drew my attention to this delightful breed.

The Polski Owczarek Nizinny is a lively, spirited breed that continually attracts new admirers from around the world.

Introduction

Since the first Polski Owczarek Nizinny (PON) or Polish Lowland Sheepdog left the borders of its native Polish territory in the early 1970s, interest in the breed worldwide has grown steadily. PONs are now a truly international breed - in Europe, the Americas, Africa and Asia. Dedicated groups of breeders in many countries have worked hard to safeguard the physical and mental soundness of the breed and to protect the breed from commercialism.

The PON is a fascinating breed to own, not always easy, but always challenging. This medium sized, shaggy sheepdog has developed its unique character and working abilities through years of usefulness to the Polish people. Today it is a loyal companion, a great friend, a tireless worker, a child's 'buddy' and a content, but watchful housedog.

This book has been written with breeders, exhibitors and dedicated PON enthusiasts in mind. It is not meant to be a practical 'how to' book for those new to the breed. There are many excellent specialist books available on breeding, rearing, showing and keeping dogs. There are two specialist PON books, currently available in English, which also cover these areas in some depth. I hope that this book may give readers a greater understanding of the breed - its form, function, character, mentality and place in Polish history. Therefore, it examines in detail the development of the breed in Poland from the earliest days to the present and does not focus, in any depth, on other countries, kennels or breeders. The majority of photographs are of Polish dogs with an exception made to feature some from my own kennel and a few from across Europe. It was my intention to use as many photographs of Polish PONs as possible, although I acknowledge that there are some excellent dogs, bred and shown outside of Poland.

Dog show in Krakow, 1968: Finka-Buba z Psiego Raju, Chmurka spod Zagla, Doman z Kordegardy, Cuma spod Zagla, Dux spod Zagla, Cwal spod Zagla.

Throughout the book I refer to the Polski Owczarek Nizinny or Polish Lowland Sheepdog as the PON, the abbreviation by which they are internationally known.

Without some human intervention, particularly before, during and after the war, the PON may not have survived to today, but it is my fear that the same human intervention may change the breed from its true Polish type. This book is my way of saying stop, think and act in the best interest of the PONs and remember the breed's value to the Polish people, which spans hundreds of years. It is their breed, we are just custodians of it.

1. The History of the Breed

The Polski Owczarek Nizinny (PON) or Polish Lowland Sheepdog belongs to the group of medium sized, European sheepdogs. This group is found on the mountain foothills and lowland plains from the eastern fringes of Russia to the western tip of France.

There is much debate over their origin and some researchers consider that the breed's ancestors were the shaggy coated, medium sized Tibetan dogs, ancestors of today's Tibetan Terriers. Most modern breeds can find their origins in Asia, being introduced to the west and south of Europe by successive waves of nomadic shepherding tribes on migrations from the east with their flocks and dogs.

In 1897 Pierre Megnin perfected a method of classification for dogs, originally devised by Cuvier in 1800. From basic anatomy, dogs were divided into four broad morphological types: Lupoids, Molossoids, Braccoids and Graioids.

The pastoral breeds of Europe, that can trace their roots back to the nomadic herders and early settlers, fall mainly into two of these types: Lupoids and Molossoids. Megnin describes Lupoids as having a head the shape of a horizontal pyramid with straight ears and a narrow elongated nose. The lips were small and tight, with the upper lips not extending beyond the base of the gums. Molossoids, according to Megnin, have a bulky and globular head with drooping ears, a short muzzle and long and thin lips. These dogs had massive bodies and were usually large framed.

Of the two distinctive types of pastoral breeds that emerged in Europe, the smaller, often heavy coated types that were used mainly for herding, fall in to the 'lupoid' group. The larger flock guardians, the mastiffs (from the Latin 'massivus' meaning massive) were of the 'molossoid type'.

A distinctive dividing line cannot be drawn between the two types because of the degree of mixed ancestry, but most European pastoral breeds fall into one category or the other. It is interesting to note that generally lupoids are found in lowland or valley regions and molossoids in mountainous areas.

THE NOMADIC PASTORALISTS

The history of the Polish Lowland Sheepdog, and indeed of all dogs, coincides with the history of man. It was during the eighth and seventh millennia B.C. that man first began to domesticate sheep and goats within the region of Western Asia. Whenever and wherever tribes migrated their valuable flock guardians went with them. Ray Coppinger, in his excellent book *Dogs - A Startling New Understanding of Canine Origin, Behavior and Evolution*, calls it 'transhumance' and asserts that the flock guardians developed wherever transhumance took place. He adds that both the herding dogs and guarding dogs were raised in the same environment, pastures, and responded to the same stimulus i.e. sheep, but in different ways.

It seems evident that these breeds all had in common their general appearance, protective instincts and presence with the Indo-European settlers.

Dr. Sandor Palfalvy's *The Origin and Migrations of the Hungarian Shepherd's Dog* points out important archaelogical findings that proved the ancestors of the Kuvaszok (plural of Kuvasz) resided in ancient Sumer over seven thousand years ago. In this area of Mesopotamia (now Iraq), the names of sheepdogs, common in Hungary today, have been found in the writings of the Sumerians.

There is one inscription that mentions a stock rearing establishment with 6 'Kumundry' (Komondors), two flocks of

The PON's general appearance is of a strong, compact dog.
Photo John Hartley.

sheep, a head of cattle and 3 'puly' (Puli). Herding tribes from the Dunar and Dnepr territories, originating in the Middle East, migrated to the old Polish territory during Neolithic times, and bone fragments found in various regions of Poland suggests that they kept medium sized dogs.

Coppinger believes that because the two types (flock herders and flock guarders) behave differently in the same environment, then the difference must be genetic. He describes types, not breeds….types being all those across Europe that look similar and do similar jobs…breeds being those that have been isolated from transhumance and bred within a closed gene pool.

Certainly over time specific breeds were developed as a result of groups of dogs being bred in isolation once a more settled form of stock rearing was established, fitting Coppinger's theory. The first evidence of stock rearing in Polish documents stem from the 13th

Century and mention farms keeping 200 to 300 sheep. It seems fair to assume that some type of sheepdog would have been working with these flocks.

The development of the small herding breeds almost certainly ran parallel to that of the large flock guardians, suffering the same hardships and lifestyle. The advancement of these breeds was dependent on the movement of herds along the various trade routes of Asia and Europe, over many centuries.

Across Europe two distinctive types of sheepdogs developed, working in tandem, in virtually every European country - the larger flock guardian, often white or wolf grey in colour, and the smaller, equally tough sheepdog. These working partners developed into many breeds recognisable today - the Pyrenean Mountain dog and the Pyrenean Sheepdog, the Estrela Mountain Dog and the Cao da Serra, the Hungarian Kuvasz and the Puli, the Tatra Moutain Dog and the PON.

The smaller sheepdogs displayed the similar characteristics of being strong and stocky for their size, very agile, extremely intelligent with excellent memories. They were faithful companions with a natural distrust of strangers, fairly resistant to illness and capable of thriving on low quality diets.

The differences that developed in these sheepdogs can be seen in size, coat, build, set of ears and tails. Coats vary from silky to coarse or corded, ears can be pricked, pendulous or drooping and tails are straight and carried low, curled and carried high, naturally bobtailed or in more recent times, docked. Despite these variations, similarities in temperament and working ability are very evident.

Although shepherds may not have consciously bred for 'type' as modern breeders do, some breeding for preferred characteristics would have occurred, although the animal's ability to work would have remained paramount. Physical exaggeration does not occur in these breeds as the shepherds needed entirely functional dogs.

Sasquehanna Kubrak Ponadto, owner Katja Jasica. PONs are agile, intelligent and stocky.

PONs are fresh air dogs and resistant to a variety of climatic conditions.

Along with the selective breeding of stock, the pastoral nomads selected for desirable attributes in their dogs. A good sheepdog needed to be fast, sturdy and strong in character. Hardiness was essential; a sheepdog may be left to remain with the flock for many days, with or without human assistance. They needed to be an effective guard against predators but to also have the ability to work quietly and efficiently. The sheepdog should be able to show initiative, be quick to learn and to have a calm, placid nature in the presence of humans. Their role, the climate and the terrain also demanded excellent feet, tough frames, weatherproof coats, strength, good hearing, keen eye sight and great robustness.

THE EARLY POLISH SHEEPDOG

A written note from the 16th century confirms the existence of a valuable working shaggy sheepdog. The reference is found in P.O.Wilson's book entitled *The Bearded Collie*. According to a document from a trade transaction dated 1514, there were six Polish sheepdogs on board a ship that sailed from Gdansk to Scotland. The merchant, Kazimierz Grabski, intended to exchange grain for sheep. The dog's role was to separate 20 sheep from a flock of sixty and presumably to pen them aboard. The Scottish shepherd was so impressed by the practical working ability of the dogs that he offered to exchange more sheep and they agreed to trade two bitches and one dog for a ram and a ewe. It appears that six dogs sailed from Gdansk, and the three that remained in Scotland are thought to have helped to shape the modern day Bearded Collie.

In the deeds of the Zamoyski family's estate, where sheep farming had existed on a large scale for many hundreds of years, there is a reference to herding dogs. From an entry in 1775 we learn that in Stroza village, seven dogs guarded a flock of 934 sheep and in Wilkolaz village, three dogs helped with 335 sheep.

Smok z Kordegardy, the foundation of the present day PON.

These estates supported sheep farming across the Lublin region and no doubt also supported the development of a suitable dog to tend them.

The next mention we have about a medium size herding dog with profuse hair and a short tail living and working in Polish territory comes from a nature publication by a zoologist, the priest Jan Kluk (1779), from the parish of Ciechanowiec.

In his four volume work he wrote "..apart from people at the sheep byre, there should also be good dogs… and as the larger dogs are for security against marauding predators, so the 'poodles' are very handy, almost guessing the shepherd's thoughts in turning, bunching etc. of the sheep, so it is well if one of them is included amongst the (big) shepherd dogs".

The author calls the small, indigenous shaggy sheepdogs 'poodles' presumably as a reference to the old German 'shepherd's poodle', a dog which was described as distinguished by its abundant coat, mostly white colouration and short tail. When listing breeds that he knew, Kluk wrote "the commonest modest poodles, which are very shaggy, are best disposed to learn anything".

In another book *Zoology - Animal Book for National Schools* (1789) Kluk observes that people tried to breed dogs according to similar characteristics "...people having noted certain external peculiarities, for example the shortness of tail, variety of coat, a different shape of muzzle etc, do not miss a chance to try and multiply such a strain".

Small sheepdogs worked on the pastures of the great estate of Anna Jablonowska in Podlasie, a region in Eastern Poland. In her *General regulations for the overseers of my domain* (written between 1783 and 1785) she ordered that up to 1000 sheep, three men, two small dogs and two large dogs should be kept to farm and manage the estate. She also passed comment on the superb working qualities of the smaller dogs.

Jan Kluk was known to use the extensive zoological library at Siemiantycze, which belonged to Princess Jablonowska and it is likely that his knowledge of stock rearing and the pastoral dogs was shaped by the practices at her estate. Already perhaps, the ancestor of the modern PON, is a valued and valuable working asset in the Podlasie region in the 18th century.

Oskar Kolberg (1814-1890), a Polish folklorist, underlines the significance of sheep farming in the Podlasie and Lublin regions. He describes the village dogs as medium sized, hairy, sharp and barking a lot. The farmers used them to chase animals and geese off the land and the peasants sometimes used them to chase and catch small game.

PONs displaying their versatility and capacity to learn and work.

I have seen myself the speed and cunning which one young bitch displayed in catching small birds and rabbits in my garden, regularly darting into undergrowth and flushing them out. This same bitch has also displayed great skill in finding her own food - from stripping plums from the branches of a tree to digging up potatoes from the earth.

The author of a *Breeding and Veterinary Guide for Farmers* (1839) writes that the sheepdogs of the time are of a medium size, good mannered and help the shepherds. Lyszkowski also notes that it is important to keep the breed pure to preserve herding instincts and abilities, and that the dogs should always be active alongside the flock.

Further descriptions of the 19th century 'Polish' sheepdogs appear in Jozef Wyzycki's *Science of Domestic Animal Breeding* (1838) and Stanislaw Rowienski's *Handbook on Dogs* (1893), both describe some variety in the herding dogs but make the same observations that they were medium sized with a narrow head and pointy muzzle, pricked ears and black, brown or dappled (speckled) in colour. In addition, Rowienski comments that the tails are either curled up or bobtailed.

In a few 19th century issues of books dedicated to the German Shepherd by Stephanitz, the PON is described as an established breed occurring in Polish and Pomerania territory; it is long-coated, white and of medium size.

Completing our picture of an early Polish sheepdog is the woodcut in 1882 by Stanislaw Maslowski entitled *'The Shepherd Boy'*. It shows a boy with a small bobtailed dog, surely an ancestor of the present day PON.

The difficult physical and environmental conditions in the old Polish territory no doubt encouraged the development of a sheepdog which could thrive on a meagre diet, had a strong resistance to different climatic conditions, with extremes of heat and cold, and a resistance to disease and illness. Many of these same features can still be observed in the breed. Today's PON is relatively resistant to disease, stubborn, persistent, adaptable, works untiringly and is vigilant to every sight, sound and smell. His natural intelligence never fails to surprise those humans that surround him.

Both herding and guarding ability were considered of equal importance. We can assume that it would not have been unusual for two or three PONs to work together, without a shepherd present, through out the day and night. They are certainly very much a 'pack' breed and quick to recognize their own type when in mixed canine company. From literature we know that the PON assisted people in driving, herding, and protecting the farm animals (sheep, cattle and geese) and then guarding the farm house during the night.

In his article published in *Pies #6, 254, 1995*, Prof. Franciszek Kobrynczuk states that it 'is because of such working abilities and utility features; (that) today's PONs are also excellent in, and have a passion to do, any kind of work or competitive play'.

So here we come full circle with the PON and his history, with the breed club in Poland considering establishing a working test to ensure that the working ability and versatility of the breed is not lost in favour of a show dog or a sofa dog. Certainly, in many countries, you can find PONs doing obedience, agility and tracking, many with championship qualifications. One PON in the USA has titles in all three and qualifies for an overall Versatility Companion Dog title. Briards cannot claim an FCI International Champion of Beauty title without passing a working qualification, maybe we will see the same introduced for PONs.

2. The Early Pioneers

In the 19th Century, dog shows were organized as part of farm animal fairs to help popularize the valuable herding sheepdogs. The first Warsaw show of livestock in 1881 featured just one such dog; the catalogue from 1882 lists four Hungarian sheepdogs. With the decline in sheep rearing at the start of the 20th century, came the decline of the shaggy sheepdog.

But the earlier dogs had not gone unnoticed. Countess Czetwertynska- Grocholska from the Radzyn district had bought a few dogs from farmers to start her own kennel (z Planty). She showed two of the first PONs in 1924, at a show in Warsaw for Poulty, Pigeons and Dogs. At this time there was no breed standard as we know it and the dogs did not have pedigrees.

At the same time mother and daughter, Wanda and Roza Zoltowskie from Milanow, relatives of the Countess, established a kennel (Milanowa) using dogs bred by Ms. Czetwertynska-Grocholska. From this point up to WWII 19 litters of PON puppies were born in the z Planty and Milanowa kennels. The most influential males were Sep and Wykop, while Fryga and Fajka were successful brood bitches. Altogether, from these two kennels, 17 Polish Sheepdogs were exhibited at shows from 1927 to 1937.

In 1937 the Working Dogs Society put a notice in their official paper 'Moj Pies' ('My Dog') about a research programme on the breed, looking for information on dogs living in the country with farmers, regardless of known pedigrees.

In this same magazine in 1939, Roza Zoltowska wrote "This breed proved to be very strong because in spite of longstanding neglect at the hands of peasants, the breed type remained uniform. The puppies in our kennel's 12 year history were always consistent in type and colour. Initially the size of the dog was 30-40cms; now

Arak Greps z Kordegardy

after several generations it is 60 cms. The coat is usually white with biscuit (pale fawn) markings on the back and ears. In our kennel sheepdogs display various abilities. They are used for herding sheep and cattle as well as guarding. They are also very pleasant house pets. One of our dogs turned out to be an excellent wild boar hunter. They are characteristically faithful, intelligent, brave and vigilant. They also have an excellent sense of smell".

Wanda Zoltowska described two types of sheepdogs in her kennel at Milanowo, "The first was an almost square dog, with a broad chest and back, strong legs, a round head, short muzzle and rather short ears. It was tailless. The coat formed a parting along its back, the legs were very well furnished and the hair on its head was abundant, falling over its eyes".

This description is not far removed from giving an impression of a modern day PON.

The second type was "a rectangular dog, with not a very broad chest and back, very strong legs, taller than the first type. Its head was longer and ear flap larger. This type of puppy rarely had a short tail and always had black noses. Their coats were more wavy, the back parting was indistinct, their heads were less hairy and the pale fawn patches occurred rarely".

Again, there are points here that fit the modern breed very well too and some amalgamation of these two types leads us to a medium sized, shaggy, slightly rectangular but very muscular sheepdog.

Although not registered in the Pure Breed Kennel Club (Zwiazek Hodowcow Psow Rasowych) they were shown and the dog named Fajkus represented the breed at the National Dog Show in Poznan in 1929.

From 1930 onwards the dogs were shown every year in Warsaw and both kennels exhibited their dogs under the name 'Polish Sheepdogs'. In 1938, members of the Working Dogs Society voiced their desire to register dogs of the domestic lowland sheepdog type. These plans were not realised due to the onset of the Second World War.

In her paper *Owczarki Nizinne z Milanowa*, Wanda Zoltowska recounts the story of her bitch Psyche, who would warn everyone of the impending peril of the wartime bombardments of Warsaw, allowing them to seek shelter from the explosions, demonstrating the breed's unique abilities.

The kennel z Planty lasted until 1941 and Milanowa until 1944, no doubt victims of the War. Only two dogs of the z Milanowa kennel survived the War, one of which - Tuska z Milanowa - eventually settled in Krakow.

The Post-War Revival

After WWII, in the magazine Pies no. 1, 1950, under the heading "Polski Owczarek Nizinny", the idea of establishing the breed was again proposed. The Polish Kennel Club appealed to its readers to submit information about the Polish Lowland Sheepdog breed so that it could be recreated and preserved. The appeal was illustrated with pictures of the dogs of Milanowa, including one of Tuska and her puppies. The announcement read:

"The Polish Lowland Sheepdog is our second native breed, which - unfortunately - seems to have become extinct during the last war. It might be possible however, that such dogs could be found somewhere in the country, where they are not recognized as pure bred. Should this happen, the organization is extremely interested in rescuing the breed and supporting it to full recognition. Typically these dogs are smaller than the Tatra sheepdog, measuring approximately 45 cms, head covered with long hair. Usually white but grey and fawn specimens occur".

The newly established Polish Kennel Club branch in Bydgoszcz played an important role in the breed's restitution. Local herding dogs bearing much resemblance to the pre-war shaggy sheepdogs were registered by Maria Dubrowinowa from Bydgoszcz and already in that same region, the first registered kennel of PONs, 'z Babiej Wsi', owned by Mrs. Kusinowicz, had been established in 1945. She was not a large breeder and between September 1945 and March 1956 only a few dogs were born and registered under this affix. These were Bies, Bystra, Bajda, Szlem, the littermates Czar, Czart and Czeri, Dukat and Diuna and from the last litter, Erga.

The breed drew the attention of another dog fancier - Dr. Danuta Hryniewicz. Her kennel was 'Kordegarda'. In 1953, three lowland sheepdogs were presented at the 1st Pomeranian Dog Show held in Bydgoszcz. Two years later there was a group of eight dogs

Czar z Babiej Wsi

and eight bitches exhibited. When developing the first outline breed standard in 1956, Maria Dubrowinowa based it on, among other dogs, Smok z Kordegardy, recognized by Lubomir Smyczynski as an ideal representative of the breed.

In her excellent work on the lines of sires and dams used in the breeding of the post-war PONs and the breed's restoration, Mrs Barbara Larska states that two dogs - Smok z Kordegardy (1949) and Szlem z Babiej Wsi (1949) - and one bitch - Bajda z Babiej Wsi (1948) were the key foundation PONs.

This period was the beginning of a somewhat slow start until the 1970s, when there is significant development in the breed.

Dr Danuta Hryniewicz with Hajda and Isia z Kordegardy

THE KORDEGARDA KENNEL

After the war, Danuta Hryniewicz had settled in the coastal village of Leba. Working as a vet, she came across a shepherd on an old estate near Lebork, whose dogs bore a resemblance to those she had seen in the pre-war years around Poznan and Lwow. She asked the farmer to keep her a puppy from a future litter from his two dogs, Kurta and Laska. In 1949 Laska, who was quite old by now, whelped one puppy, this was Smok z Kordegardy (born 22.12.49); as Dr Hryniewicz was involved in breeding other breeds at this time, she placed Smok with a local shepherd and he became well known for his excellent herding ability.

It appears that the article in Pies caught her attention and her local kennel club put her in touch with Mrs Kusionwicz and her kennel z Babiej Wsi. In 1955 Dr Hryniewicz bought two dogs from z Babiej Wsi called Dukat and Diuna. Smok returned to her kennel and in 1954 she also obtained Wiga, a bitch from Krakow, who was very similar to the pre-war dogs and probably linked to the early

PONs of Planta and Milanowa. Three Kordegarda litters were bred in 1956 - two from Smok and Diuna and one from Smok and Wiga. From the first pairing she kept Kuma, Nerpa and Niwa and from Wiga's litter Wiga Wara. Initially the dogs were white and grey and white. Wiga Wara, bred back to Smok, produced the black and white male Re-Mis.

Between 1956-59, Smok sired 10 litters and the breed was, and is, inbred on Smok. Inbreeding was a necessity; Dr Hryniewicz had to use concentrated inbreeding and did not record any bad results in the litters produced. She maintains that she owes the success of her kennel and breeding programme to Smok. She asserted that as a highly homozygous dog, he passed all his virtues on to his progeny and set the foundation for the future.

Progress was slow. In 1956, 9 dogs were registered and numbers began to increase slightly. In 1958 the first fully certified (registered) litter came from Dukat and Niwa and

The famous Ch Doman z Kordegardy, grandson of Smok.

included the famous white dog Arak Greps. The other important litter that year came from Smok and Kuma, which included Inkluz and Iwa.

In 1962 the first puppy, Ryza, was born at the z Atlanty kennel. Her sire was Czart Kita Lado z Antalka (bred from two Kordegarda dogs) and the dam was Muszka Rara. Muszka Rara was from a bitch called Bebi, believed to be unrelated to the Kordegarda line, but about whom no details are recorded. Muszka Rara had a further five litters at 'z Atlanty' but it appears that her line then vanished from the breed's gene pool.

In a publication about PONs in 1958, Danuta Hryniewicz commented on their characteristics: " it is a medium size dog, strong, muscular, stocky, alert, intelligent, suspicious of strangers, perceptive, sharp minded, good memory, requires no management, resistant to disease and not peculiar to food. An abundant coat serves as protection from rain and frost. He is widely utilized and popular on straight, territorial Pomeranian planes as a herding dog and a guard of farmers' houses. When moved to urban areas he will be a smart babysitter, a cheerful companion for a walk, alert, and eager to protect the home in which he lives." In the same year she bred her first litter with full pedigrees.

FEDERATION CYNOLOGIQUE INTERNATIONALE (FCI) RECOGNITION

The provisional breed standard was prepared by Maria Dubrowinowa in 1956. The Polish Kennel Club Board of Directors met in Poznan on May 9, 1959 to approve the standard and the FCI officially recognized the breed. The standard was approved by the FCI in 1961 and registered as number 251.

Dr Hryniewicz purchased Certa z Melna (born 14.08.59) sired by Krokus z Kordegardy (Smok x Diuna) and from Erga z Babiej

Int.PL.CS Ch Doman z Kordegardy by Lider z Kordegardy ex Certa z Melna

Wsi. Certa became an influential brood bitch producing, amongst others, the magnificent Int. PL. CS Ch. Doman z Kordegardy, a direct descendant from Smok. He dominated breeding in the early 70's.

In 1961 Amok Moniek was bred by Hanna Rek in Gdansk, from Inkluz z Kordegardy and Harfa z Kordegardy. He became the breed's first Polish champion and the first international champion, from any breed, bred and handled by Poles. He was also World Winner at Brno in 1965. There, for the first time, Poland was represented on an international arena by several PONs. Nine were shown and all received excellent gradings.

Ch Szelma z Kordegardy also received the World Winner title at the same show. By 1969, the Kordegarda kennels had produced some 150 puppies and 31 of them became champions.

In the early 1960s two kennels were established, which were to make their mark on the breed - 'spod Zagla' founded on Ch Garda Wtora z Kordegardy, whose litter brother Giermek was the first

Int.PL Ch Amok Moniek bred by Hanna Rek. He was the breed's first Polish champion and World Winner '65.

chocolate PON born at Kordegarda. Garda Wtora's first litter with Amok Moniek was born on 7.8.1963. The second kennel was 'z Psiego Raju'. The first registered litter from this kennel was born on 28.2.64 sired by Lider z Kordegardy and from Certa z Melna. Szelma also went to this kennel after giving litters at 'z Lagiewnickiego Boru' and 'z Kolchidy'.

The Psi Raj kennel went on to produce a well known line of influential champions including the 1975 Polish Club winner Gwarek z Psiego Raju, who became its main sire.

The Polish Lowland Sheepdog now had FCI recognition but still the breed remained quite small and one must remember the social and political restrictions of the time under Communist rule. According to Lubomir Smyczynski, a recognized authority and judge, it took 15 years after WW11 to get the breed established with several top quality dogs for breeding.

To help promote the breed the same dogs were shown around

the country. Ch Wigor Gol z Jurty (born in 1971 from Doman and Rola z Kordegardy) collected some 35 CACs. Several PONs were shown at the World Show in Budapest in 1971 and by 1975 there were 66 PON kennels in Poland, most with between one and three bitches. In that same year, 72 dogs were at the National Speciality in Bydgoszcz, best male was Gwarek z Psiego Raju and best female was Cuma spod Zagla.

In 1978 Wigor Gol z Jurty was considered by Prof. Jadwiga Dyakowska (a famous caninologist and expert on Polish breeds) as the standard of perfection for the breed.

The breed made steps outside its homeland too with the first

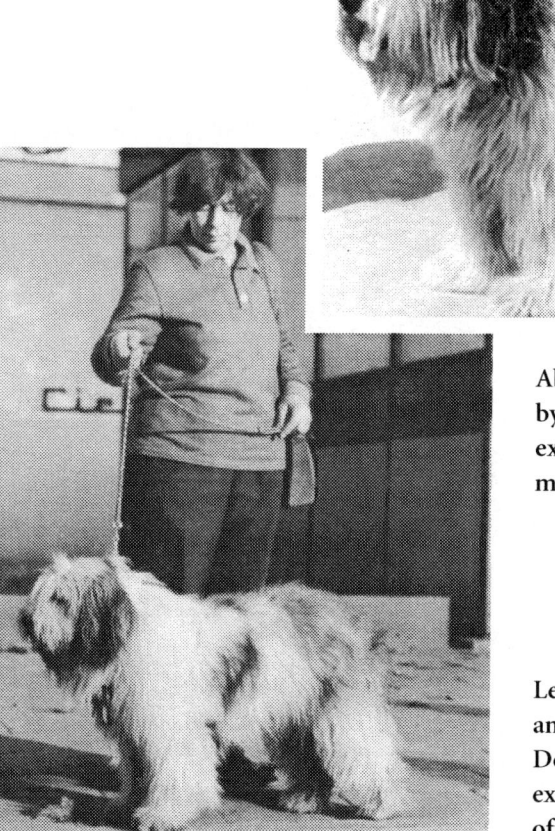

Above: Ch Wigor Gol z Jurty by Ch Doman z Kordegardy ex Ch Rola z Kordegardy, a multiple CAC winner.

Left: Dr Danuta Hryniewicz and Ch Doman z Kordegardy. Doman passed his many excellent qualities on to his offspring.

PONs imported to East Germany by Mrs Gartenschlager in the late 1960s. The first import was Czeremcha z Kolchidy (dob 23.9.67 from Amok Moniek x Szelma z Kordegardy and bred in Lodz).

From this time until the 80s Mrs Gartenschlager bred under the PON-Garten affix. In 1969 she bred Akis v PON-Garten (Doman x Czeremcha) who became an International, Polish, East German, Czech and Hungarian champion and was used at stud by 'spod Zagla', producing the Polish champions Grog and Garda. Dany v PON-Garten, born in 1974, became a Czech and Danish champion and Eicko v PON-Garten, born in 1975, became a Czech, Romanian and Hungarian champion, both were sired by Akis. In 1974 the Allgemeine Klub fur Polnische Rassehunde was founded.

In the 1970s Michel and Lucienne Jasica, who already had the

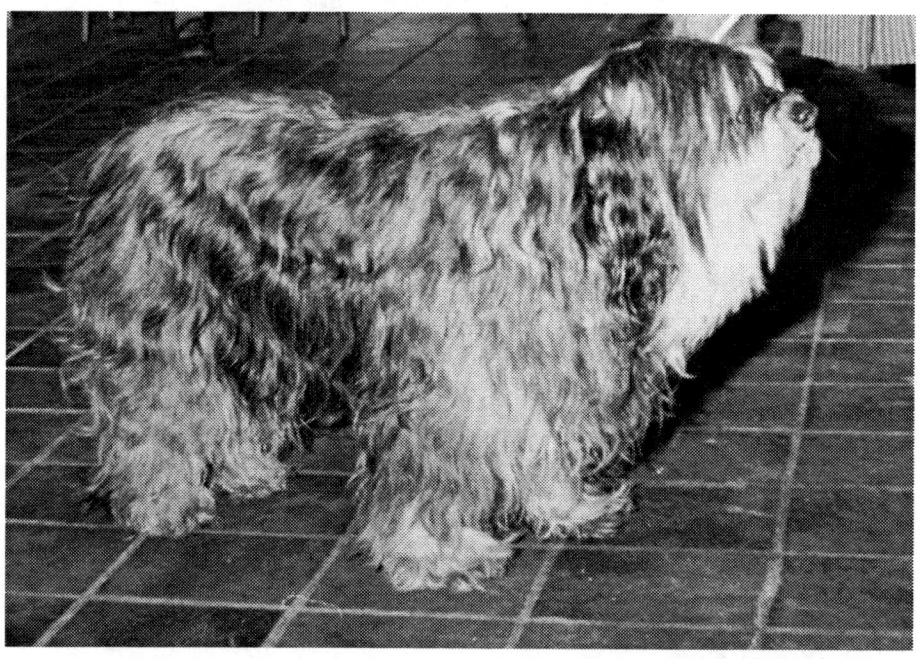

Int.B.NL.Lux Ch Zuk Urania, at the Jasica's 'van het Goralenhof' kennel, helped to promote the breed in Western Europe in the 1970s.

successful 'van het Goralenhof' kennel of Tatras and Pyrenean Mountain dogs, imported the first PONs into western Europe. These were Zuk Urania (dob 26.12.69 by Cwik spod Zagla and Arabella z Alty) and Miedza z Kordegardy (dob 14.7.70 by Doman and Beza z Lagiewnickiego Boru). The first two champions from the kennel were Vasco and Vania van het Goralenhof, litters mates born on 24.1.72 from Zuk and Miedza. Zuk Urania went on to become a Belgian, Dutch, Luxemburg and International Champion. The Jasica family promoted the breed across Western Europe and the kennel name and breeding programme continues with daughter Katja.

INTO THE '80S

In the 1980s registrations increased dramatically and by the end of the decade it was possible to see up to 80 PONs or more exhibited at shows. At the 1984 Polish National Specialty there was an entry of 135 dogs, best male was Apasz z Bankowcow and best female Arkonia z Kordegardy. This decade led to the establishment of a number of kennels that have highly influenced the breed through the 80s and 90s and well up to the present day.

It is difficult to mention a few without mentioning many, or to ignore the smaller breeders who may have only ever had a litter or two (such as z Jurty), yet produced a few special dogs whose influence is still felt today. However, I feel it is impossible not to mention four kennels from the 1980s - the 'z Gangu Dlugich' kennel of Barbara Larska, founded on Kordegardy lines and home to the influential sire Apasz z Bankowcow; the 'z Wielgowa' kennel of Janusz Zerebecki, founded almost entirely on the 'Psi Raj' dogs; the 'Kontrapunkt' kennel of Janina Staniszewska-Borkowska, whose kennel produced 19 litters between 1979 and 1989. The first litter born at Kontrapunkt was by Figaro z Jagniatkowa and Frytka z

Int.PL Ch Radosz z Psiego Raju by Ch Gwarek z Psiego Raju ex Bella z Nadwarcianskiej Doliny. Breeder T. Adamski

Left: Ch Gwarek z Psiego Raju by Witez z Kordegardy ex Rzepicha z Psiego Raju

Right: 1987 Club winner Ch Palasz z Wielgowa by Ch Radosz z Psiego Raju ex Garstka Sagittarius

Kordegardy. Figaro was a son of Wega Gamma z Jurty, litter sister to Wigor Gol; Frytka was from a direct line to Smok and Diuna's first litter back in 1956. The fourth kennel is z Zeriby, home to Ch Matros z Kordegardy and Jurand Grenada, sire of Ch Apasz z Bankowcow, Ch Igor z Zeriby, Ch Lancet z Zeriby and Golf z Zeriby, amongst others.

The PON reached the UK in 1985 when Megan Butler (Megsflocks) imported the first 6 dogs from the de Halkaza kennel of Zenon Mossakowski in Belgium (the PONs descending in part from Lucienne Jasica's 'van het Goralenhof' kennel). There were three males Jucha, Jonasz and Jaki da and one female Janka, plus the male Jurista and his litter sister Jasna, from a second litter. The breed was first exhibited in 1986 at the National Working Breeds Society and between 1985 and 1991 there were 42 imports in to the country. In 1997 the breed achieved full KC recognition.

In the USA, a Bearded Collie breeder, Moira Morrison had imported Bundz ze Starego Lupkowa and Fajerka z Kordegardy in 1979. It was from Moira that Betty Augustowski got her first PON, Pan Vladek, in 1982 and in 1983 Krymka z Kordegardy arrived in whelp. Under Betty's guidance the PON flourished in the USA and achieved full AKC recognition in August 2001. Betty was made an honourary life member of the PON Club at the 2003 National Specialty in Lodz, in recognition of her service to the breed.

Today the breed has stretched far and wide around the world - from South America to South Africa, to the Far East and Australasia and across the whole of Europe. Behind every single PON, in every single country, lies one dog - Smok z Kordegardy.

3. The Breed Standard

The first standard for the breed was approved by the FCI in 1961 and registered as number 251. The FCI accepted modifications to it in 1963, 1973 and 1989. In 1989 the PON Club of Poland proposed changes to the height at withers, and descriptions for the tail and feet, which were accepted.

At the Breed Congress in Lodz, September 2003, the PON Club proposed some slight changes in wording to the standard and presented, for the first time, a commentary explaining each point in detail, to accompany the standard. The breed standard committee which drew this up comprised Dr Tomasz Borkowski, Mrs Barbara Larska, Dr Anna Dominiak and Mr Andrzej Stepinski. It is Poland's wish that all countries use this standard and this seems a sensible way forward for the breed's continued worldwide development.

Two main issues led to the Congress at Lodz; firstly not all countries are using the same standard and although the differences may appear slight to the eye on reading, the difference in the PONs being promoted was much greater; secondly many articles were being written evaluating the breed, some contradictory, and it was felt that Poland should issue the standard view of their breed - "It is the wish of the Polish Kennel Club that there be one official interpretation and that all discrepancies can be laid aside so that PONs will be upheld to the same standards all over the world". This seems a totally fair request and an eminently sensible one; for this reason the standard included on the next few pages is the FCI standard.

The two countries mentioned for slight standard differences were the USA and UK and it is true that the standards do vary slightly. Both countries took their standards from the FCI 251 standard but did not adopt them verbatim. In the UK standard the height for males differs to that of the FCI and an error in translation led to the word 'amble' being included under movement, rather than 'pace'. The Polish word 'posuwisty' means 'with long easy strides' but in the dictionary it is also 'at an amble'. The Polish standard at the time said 'Ruch: Swobodny, posuwisty step lub klus' - 'Gait: Free, with long easy strides, walking or trotting pace'.

This error came to light following an article on the breed and its movement by American writer Robert Cole, published in Dog News, Dec 07, 2001. The article was based on the AKC standard approved in January 1997. Cole picks out what he calls 'three controversial statements' where the AKC standard differs to that of the FCI, and therefore of Poland.

Both the UK and USA standards use the word 'cobby', the FCI standard says 'compact'. In Harry Spira's *Canine Terminology* the author states that cobby means compact, thick set, chunky and relatively short both in body length as well as height. To many people 'cobby' means square, whereas, when applied to the PON, it clearly means compact. Neither short legged nor leggy dogs should be considered as typical for the breed.

Another key difference picked out in the AKC standard was that the points of measurement for the 9:10 height:length ratio. These were incorrectly stated as being from point of wither to ground and point of wither to point of buttock. This length measurement should be taken from the point of shoulder.

Occasionally you still come across references to three sizes too. At one stage during the preparation of a provisional standard three size varieties were discussed but it was the medium size that was bred and so the original standard prepared by Maria Dubrowinowa, calls for a medium size dog. The three size varieties were Maly which is 35cms, Sredni which is 40 to 43cms and Duzy which is over 50cm, minimum 48cm, but the larger the better. The standard below includes the proposed translation changes. It is still pending FCI approval.

FCI STANDARD NO. 251.
Translation:
Mrs Peggy Davis

Origin:
Poland

Utilization:
Easy to handle and works like a sheepdog and guard dog. Moved to urban city life, he is a very good companion dog.

Classification FCI:
Group 1 Sheepdogs and Cattle Dogs
(except Swiss Cattle Dogs).
Section 1 sheepdogs.
Without working trial.

General Appearance:
The Polish Lowland Sheepdog is a dog of medium size, compact, strong, muscular, with a thick long coat. Their well groomed coat gives an attractive and interesting appearance.

Important Proportions:
The proportions of height at withers to length of body is 9:10. The ratio length of muzzle to length of skull is 1:1, however a muzzle slightly shorter than this is acceptable.

Multi champion Wiwat Pacynka with owner Anna Dominiak.

Behaviour and Temperament:

Of a lively but tempered disposition, vigilant, agile, intelligent, perceptive and gifted with a good memory, resistant to unfavourable climatic conditions.

Head:

Medium dimension, proportional and not too heavy. The thick fur on the forehead, the cheeks and the chin give the head a look of being bigger than it actually is.

Cranial Region:

Skull: Not excessively broad, slightly rounded. Frontal furrow and occipital protuberance noticeable.

Stop: Well accentuated

Facial Region:

Nose: As dark as possible in relation to the colour of the coat with large nostrils.

Muzzle: Strong, blunt, with straight nasal bridge.

Lips: Fitting well; their edges are of the same colour as the nose.

Jaw/Teeth: Strong jaws. Teeth strong, with scissor or level bite.

Eyes: Medium size, oval, not protruding, hazel colour, with lively and piercing look. The rims of the eyelids are dark.

Ears: Hanging, set moderately high, of medium size, heart-shaped, wide at the base; the fore edge is close against the cheeks and mobile.

Neck:

Of medium length, strong, muscular, without dewlap, carried rather horizontally

Body:

Outline: Rectangular rather than square

Withers: Well accentuated.

A beautiful head study of the world famous multi champion Malina z Gangu Dlugich, European Winner '02 and World Winner '03.

The desired outline of the PON - a well set neck, marked withers, level topline and short, slightly sloping croup.

Back: Flat, well muscled.

Loin: Broad, well fused.

Croup: Short, slightly truncated.

Chest: Deep, of medium width, ribs quite well sprung, neither flat nor barrel-shaped.

Underline and Belly: Curving towards the hindquarters.

Tail:
Naturally short, stumpy, tailless, very shortly docked tail. Undocked quite long and very hairy tail. At rest the tail hangs; if the dog is alert the tail gaily curves over the back, never curled or lying on the back. Naturally undocked tail of medium length, carried in different manners.

Limbs:
Forequarters: Seen in profile and from the front: vertical and straight. Stance well balanced due to a strong skeleton (bone structure).

Shoulders: Broad, of medium length, oblique, clean cut, very muscular.

Pastern: Slightly slanting in relation to the forearm.

Forefeet: Oval, tight, slightly arched toes with hard pads. Nails short and preferably dark.

Am Ch Walor z Gangu Dlugich, a medium sized dog of great strength and substance. Breeder Barbara Larska.

Hindquarters:

Seen from behind: Vertical, well angulated.

Thighs: Broad and muscular.

Hocks: Well accentuated.

Hind feet: Compact, oval shape.

Gait/Movement:

Effortless and ground covering. Smooth walk or trot with good reach and drive, often pacing.

Skin:

Tight fitting without any folds.

COAT

Hair:

The whole body is covered with dense, thick, and profuse hair and soft undercoat. Hair should be straight, though slightly wavy is acceptable. The hair falling from the forehead covers the eyes in a characteristic manner.

Colour:

All colours are acceptable.

Size:

Height at withers: Males: 45-50cm Females: 42-47cm

The dog must retain the type of a working dog, therefore their size must not go down below the standard. They must be neither weak nor delicate.

Faults:

Any departure from the standard should be considered a fault and the seriousness with which the fault should be regarded should be in exact proportion to its degree.

N.B. Male animals should have two apparently normal testicles fully descended into the scrotum.

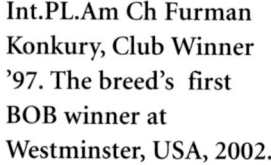

Int.PL.Am Ch Furman Konkury, Club Winner '97. The breed's first BOB winner at Westminster, USA, 2002.

Two PONs from the Wielgowa kennel of Janusz Zerebecki. Ch. Rapier owned by Birgit Roese and six month old Imbir owned by Karen Robinson and myself. Both dogs are demonstrating good reach and drive and correct toplines.

All colours and markings are accpetable and all considered equally beautiful!

Comments about the Standard

It was a huge task to put together the proposed commentary to accompany the standard and the document, in translated form, is some 18 pages. It is hoped that it will be accepted as the worldwide standard view of the breed. The purpose of this book is not to replicate discussions that have already taken place but bring together the history, facts and insights to the breed to get a complete view of this very versatile dog. Once published, reading and re-reading the standard commentary will be a must for any real breed enthusiast.

The following discussion takes its direction from the propsed Polish commentary; the comments below do not refer to any particular dog, but to the standard, and reflect many personal views.

General Appearance

You must look first and foremost at the whole dog. This does not just mean his anatomy and construction, but also his attitude and temperament. You need to stand back and look at the dog, get your hands into the coat, watch him move and weigh up the virtues rather than focus on the faults. It is often difficult not to get 'hung up' on a few points - for me it's flat withers, lack of neck, poor dipping toplines and straight stifles - but you should never focus on just a few 'faults' and disregard the whole appearance of the dog.

When I first look at a PON I am always looking for a robust, strong, typical dog, without any exaggerations when standing or moving. A dog that is balanced, slightly rectangular, muscular and hardy without being coarse. A dog that displays a free and easy gait, with plenty of scope, a straight, weatherproof coat, strong legs and feet, a dog bred for its purpose. I want an impression of strength and substance (not coarseness) in dogs and bitches. The impression of strength and substance does not come from height at withers but from width and depth of the body, overall balance and correct proportions.

Size is important and I always look to the upper medium and above in the standard and males should look like males - they must be masculine whatever their size. Proportions are important - not square, not too long, not with legs too short for its body or too leggy. Judges must pay attention to proportions - you don't want the squareness of the Bobtail or the length of the Bearded Collie. Above all, it must look like a PON!

Important Proportions

The height to length ratio is measured from the top of the wither to the ground and from the point of shoulder to point of buttock; the desired ratio is 9:10, if not, it is unbalanced. You must remember that a dog which is taller at the withers than another will also be longer in the body than the other. A dog that is 18 inches high should be 20 inches long. When you draw the proportions on a diagram you may be forgiven for thinking it looks almost square, but it is not an exact square. Optically your eye will see something different as you will see also the forechest and coat when viewing the whole dog.

The muzzle should be measured from the top of the nose to the inner corner of the eye and from there to the occipital bone. The desired ratio is 1:1, slightly shorter is acceptable but not the desired ratio. Too short a muzzle changes the whole balance of the head and the expression. I do not believe that the muzzle should be any shorter than 0.8:1.

Two typical, strong yet feminine bitches. Int.PL.Fin Ch Utopia Oligarchia, Club Winner '98, breeder & owner Andrzej Stepinski and Ch Flinkbein Ekspanat, Club Winner '01, breeder Taija Tuohilampi, owner Janusz Zerebecki.

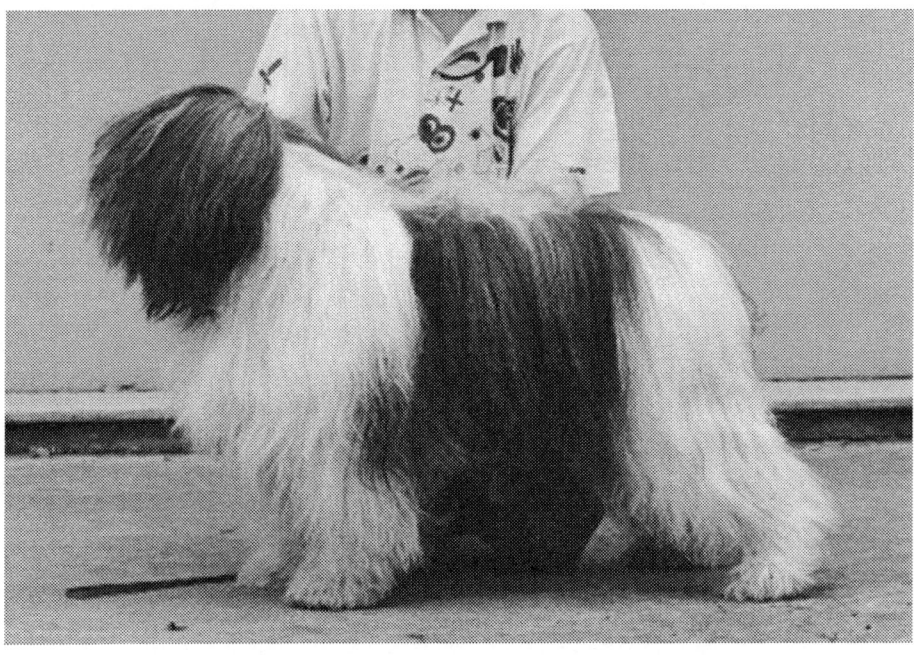

Int.PL.Fin Ch Zur z Wielgowa by Olek v.d. Widderburg ex Garstka Saggitarius.

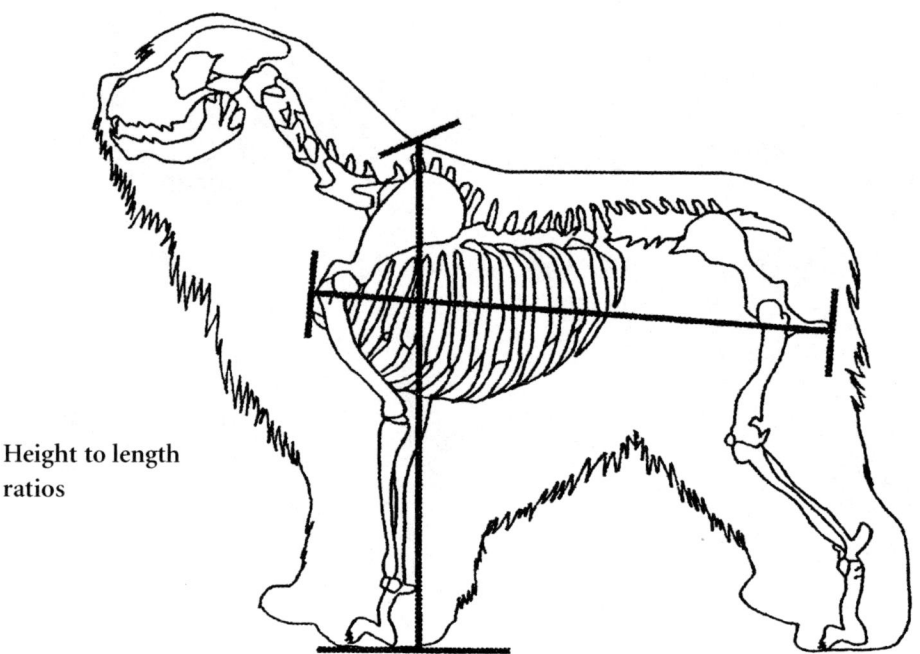

Height to length ratios

Temperament

The PON can be a well trained showdog but this does not mean that he is like a couch potato, slouching around the ring, or reminds one of a toy dog that is only missing a set of wheels, so he can be pushed around. This is a clever, perceptive dog. You can tell a PON that has a good rapport with its owner, that is stimulated, alert, lively but at the same time self controlled, you can see this in the ring.

Head

The head should appear big but be proportionate to the whole dog with a broad strong muzzle, nice big nose but not a really deep stop. The skull should be flat and medium to large but fitting the rest of the dog, that is, not too heavy as to appear unbalanced. Many judges often seem surprised when they feel the PON's skull that it is not bigger - they do not have huge skulls, the hair and the manner in which it falls makes the head look bigger than it is.

The muzzle should be broad, strong and straight, The teeth should be big, white and strong. The PON should not have narrow lower jaws or excessive flews. The eyes are oval and hazel, there is no requirement for a 'dark eye', only for the eye rims to be as dark as possible in relation to the colour of the coat. The ears are large, very mobile and close to the head and set with the base in line with the outside corner of the eye.

Neck

Medium neck means just that, not no neck at all! The PON must have a medium reach of neck, which gives the dog a visible, smooth outline and is well set; withers must be well marked, not flat, this is essential for the correct outline. It is becoming rare to see the correct shape in PONs in some countries, with many PONs having no neck and no visible withers or being flat over the withers. If the length of the whole spine (not counting tail vertebrae) is taken as 100%, the neck vertebrae are approximately 27%.

Again the eye can play optical tricks and a large head and profuse coast may make the neck seem shorter than it really is. One point that is important for me is that the head does not look as if it's set straight on the scapula, and the neck is both noticeable and muscular. A correct neck, correctly set, with well marked withers and a broad firm back gives the PON its distinct, desired and beautiful outline.

Body

The proper rectangular proportions have already been discussed. The chest should be deep, reaching to the elbow (but not more) and broad with plenty of heart and lung room, PONs should not have a narrow front and stand with their front legs close together, if the chest is correct this is impossible.

The withers should be distinct and the neck should flow into them. The withers are also wide and at their points easily two fingers width apart. The withers should be higher than the croup by on average 2%.

The PON's whole body should be broad and strong, they are broad at the withers, without a waist, broad over the loin, broad over the croup, with a strong, well muscled back and loin and the **same width** all through when viewed from above, not narrow with slab sides and no brisket. This is important for the correct topline and fluid, efficient movement; the back must be straight and strong, no dipping or rising. The croup is short and very slightly sloping, not rounded.

Tail

This is one part of the standard that is frequently under debate due to current European regulations concerning the banning of docking in some countries. Many of the pre- war and inter-war

The PON's rectangular body is broad and strong. The topline is level and strong, displaying no weakness in the back.

PONs are accepted to have had no tail or very short tails. Dr Hryniewicz has stated that Smok and Wiga were tailess and Doman had one vertebrae. Docking was introduced to help standardize the breed. In a litter of PONs it is possible to see many tail lengths, from very short to 3 or 4cms to full length. Therefore it is impossible to state that the undocked tail must be a set length. It is possible to make some statements about tail carriage from the anatomy of the PON.

Respected judge Lucienne Jasica has written "There have been many discussions about the tail of the PON. To those who are for or against, let us remember the facts. The PON is and will always be a Polish breed. It is the Polish Kennel Club that decides what their breed should look like."

Many European breeders feel that Poland, as the country of origin, should provide guidance on tails, but this is very difficult for them to do, as the PON has many natural tail lengths. For the time being you can only assume that no tail type, length or carriage is incorrect as the 'correct' tail has yet to be determined by Poland.

The view from the Lodz Congress was that when judging it is best, for now, to ignore the tail in terms of making any place decisions.

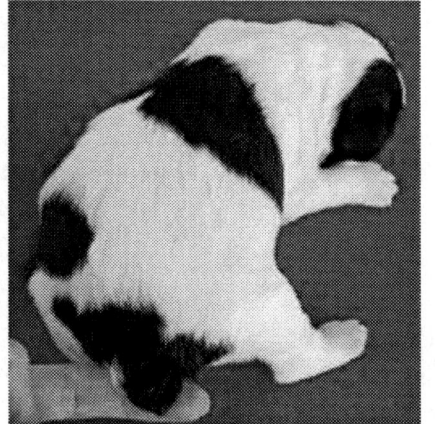

A puppy with a full tail and a naturally bobtailed puppy.

Given that European regulations could soon affect all breeders in EU countries, it would be wise to record all tail lengths at birth for future reference.

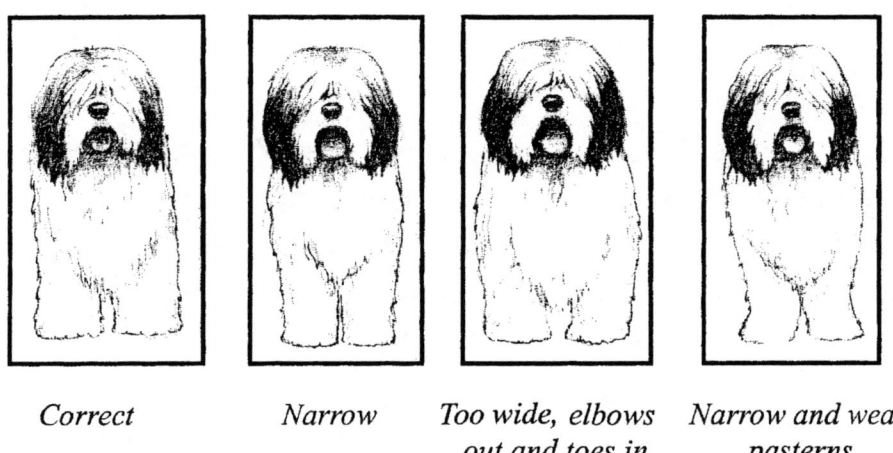

Correct   *Narrow*   *Too wide, elbows out and toes in*   *Narrow and weak pasterns*

Forequarters

They should have strong, straight bone and well padded, tight feet, pasterns are slightly sloping to allow for flexible movement and the ability to turn. The shoulders should be well muscled.

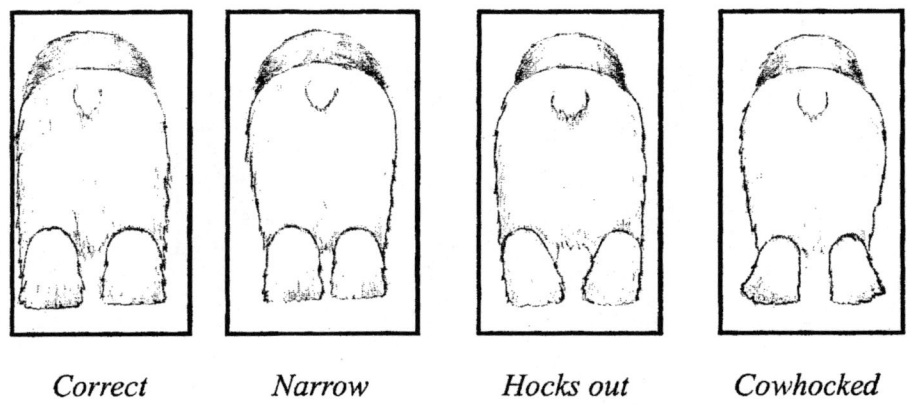

Correct   *Narrow*   *Hocks out*   *Cowhocked*

Hindquarters

The hindquarters, as with the front legs, should be parallel and muscular, hocks are well let down to allow for driving from the rear. The PON cannot function properly if it has weak hocks, cow hocks or sloppy pasterns.

Movement

PON's movement should be viewed from all angles, straight up and down and in profile. They should show reach and drive, moving with long strides, no exaggeration, no kicking up hocks, over reaching, hackneying, or paddling - a smooth, easy gait, almost effortless; it should be a joy to watch. It should be straight and parallel. As the dog moves faster there is a natural tendency for the limbs to converge. Too often I see PONs that I would describe as 'busy going nowhere' - they are taking lots of steps but not really moving forward at all, just pitterpatting along. Also it is common to see many that are close behind.

At slow speeds, they have a tendency to pace. The 'pace' is a two beat lateral gait, in which the legs on each side move back and forth exactly as a pair, causing a rolling or rocking motion.

Often you read that they should move with their head carried almost horizontally. I would counter this and suggest that a lively, alert and confident show dog may well carry its head a little higher and should not be penalized for it. The proposed commentary suggest that the head should be carried at the 10 o'clock position and the reach should be free and long with the length of the perpendicular line to the ground going from the outside corner of the eye, with the head in this position.

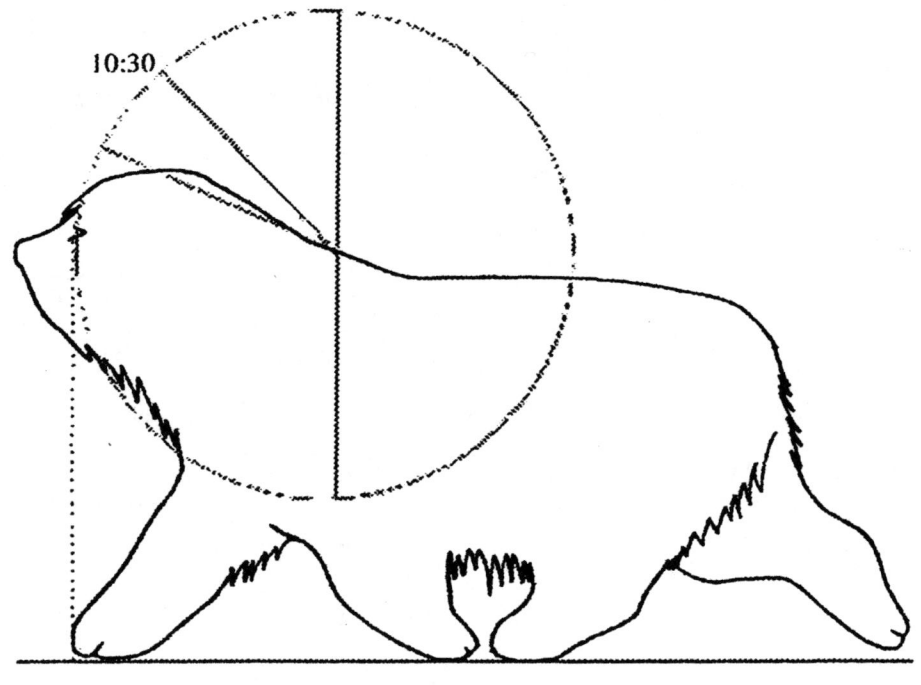

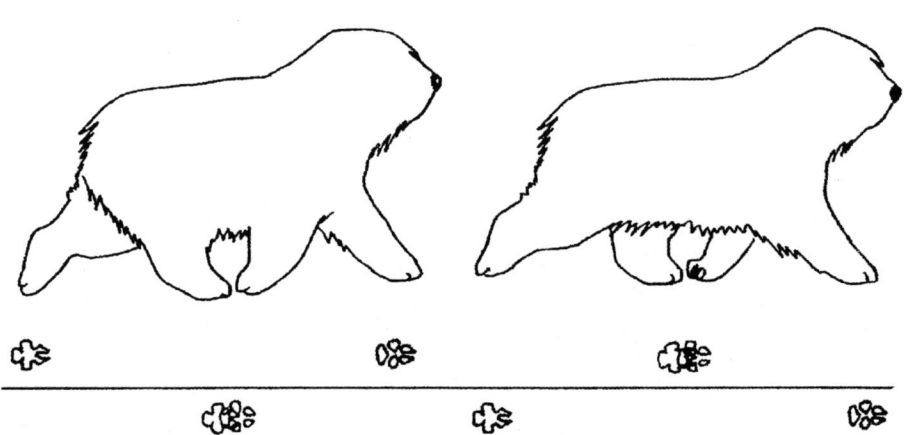

55

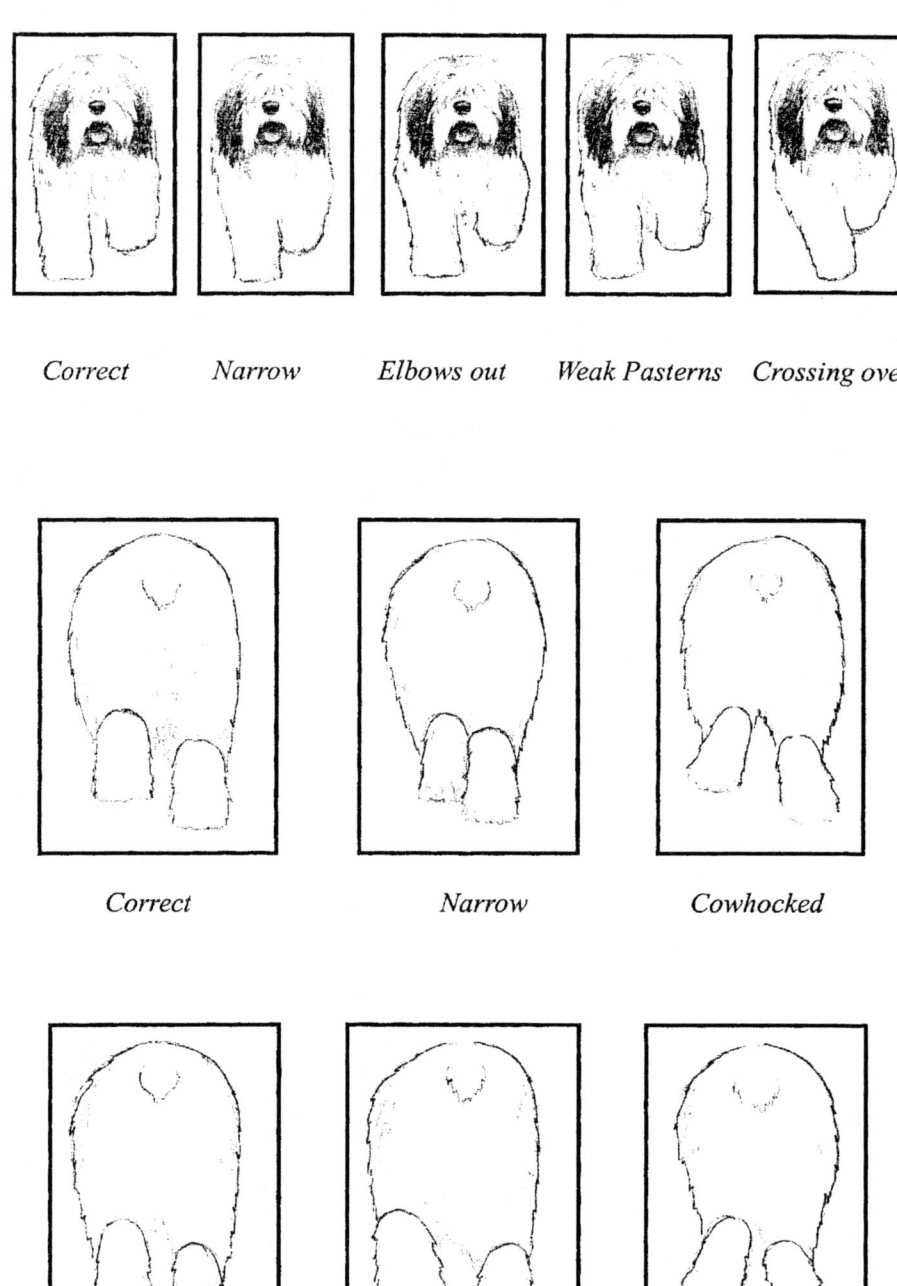

COAT

The coat should be long, straight and harsh, not woolly, silky or very wavy (a slight wave is permissible). I think it is unwise to start making allowances for poor coat quantity, quality or texture because of the colour of the dog. Whatever their colour, the coat should still be weatherproof and functional for the job they were originally bred to do. It may have some bearing on texture, but not on the amount of top coat or undercoat and the straightness of the coat. The coat should be harsh and should be the same texture and type all over, the males often have a bit of a 'ruff' - more on their neck and chests. On adult dogs the coat may be as long as 20cms or more.

Ch Mazur z Gangu Dlugich, Club Winner '04, pictured in his natural state, prior to show grooming. The PON's coat should not be excessively trimmed or sculptered with scissors.

The PON's coat is long, straight and thick, covering the entire body. It should be the same texture all over.

Colour

All colours are acceptable and no preference should be given for any colour(s) over another nor should the colour in solid dogs be expected to be even all over.

SIZE

The standard clearly states "The dog must retain the type of a working dog, therefore their size must not go down below the standard. They must be neither weak nor delicate". This is quite clear and unequivocal. I do not understand why some breeders seem to want to breed a smaller PON standing at the bottom of the standard (and promote some below it) when we are left in no doubt, that this is a medium size dog.

The PON standing at 45cms and below all too often loses bone, substance and strength and starts to look more like a Tibetan Terrier. I believe there should be more tolerance given to height measurements that are top size and up to 2cms over the standard but not 2cms below the standard. The UK standard with its lower size band for males is possibly harmful to the future of the breed.

4. Judging the Polish Lowland Sheepdog

The standard describes an ideal of the breed but is not overly comprehensive or detailed. It provides the conformation framework but it is up to the breeder and the judge to fill that framework. The perfect dog exists in the imagination and each of us will have a slightly different conception of the 'ideal PON'. The standard is there to act as a guide when breeding and judging. It still requires our own views, ideas, opinions and imagination to 'put flesh on the bones'

Really good judges are born with an eye for a dog and can spot quality, construction, movement and style in any breed. Most are not so lucky and need to study conformation to properly appreciate the way a dog is constructed, taking into account its function in life (the job it was bred for) as this affects the way it is built and the way it moves. Each breed has its own idiosyncracies that sets it apart from others, even when grouped with like breeds - the OES' rising topline and pear shape, compared with the level topline of the lean and lithe Bearded Collie.

I believe that judges must always have 'breed type' uppermost in their minds. Good judges are born not made, but that is not to say you cannot develop a breed specialism through contact with the breed, reading and listening. Breed seminars are a good place to gain in depth breed knowledge but there is a caveat - the seminar is only as good as the knowledge of the speaker, their presentation and communication skills and the quality of the dogs you get to put your hands on. Beware of heavily biased opinions! In rare or numerically small breeds judges carry a great responsibility to assess that breed correctly and to reward accordingly; judges consistently promoting untypical dogs can do a breed a great future disservice.

As Dr Carmen Battaglia says "the facts are that the judge and breeder are central to making breed improvements and there are rules that control the judging process. These rules are important because they can influence a breed's function, the quality of those that win and to some degree, the destiny of a breed".

In their excellent article *Where is Typical Movement Going?* Hans Lehtinen and Chris Lummelampi state "all too often, we seem to be using the same yardstick to measure the quality of a dog, and we are too easily impressed with flashy showmanship and clever presentation.

Someone once observed that, all too often, we believe a dog is a good mover if it covers the ground like a German Shepherd, comes and goes like a Beagle, and to top it all, has the Setter topline, the animation of a Cocker Spaniel and the general attitude of a Poodle. Never mind if it is a typical example of its breed, epitomizing its written and unwritten breed standard. Never mind if its attitude is that of a composite, outgoing, animated show dog of no particular breed type, as long as it meets the generally accepted criteria for soundness .."

When judging you should be looking for the best dog and decisions should be made on an understanding of correct type for the breed, sound anatomical construction, typical movement and typical temperament. A really good judge will also have an 'eye' for balance and quality.

One of Poland's oldest judges Zygmunt Jakubowski believes that when judging the PON, both type and working ability should be important. When there were fewer dogs at shows, judges had more time and were perhaps more thorough in their assessments. Assessing structure, movement and coat is half of the judge's task, the other half is temperament, character and behaviour, all too often overlooked.

As Andrew Brace says in his book *The Essential Guide to Judging Dogs* "the mental approach of any dog is as much a part of its breed type as head, expression, tail carriage.."

SEEING THROUGH THE COAT

Coated breeds require a different approach to smooth breeds; clever handling and grooming can obscure faults and highlight virtues and a judge needs to be aware of this.

A good judge can see the balance of body proportions but sometimes coat can be deceptive, as on the head. Muzzle to skull ratios can be measured with the thumb and index finger. I have seen judges kneel and place one hand on the point of shoulder the other at point of buttock, to help assess body proportions, there is nothing wrong with this if you can not judge by eye. After all the eye can be deceptive.

Judges forget sometimes that the proportion for length is in relation to height, a larger dog will be longer - this is a problem when some judge, they forget what ratio they are looking at - a 19inch dog will obviously look longer than an 18inch, dog (if proportioned correctly), some do not seem to appreciate this and end up placing rather square dogs. A judge should also know the measurement points too!

Look for virtues not faults. Fault judging is not good practice as no dog is ever perfect. However when assessing virtues and faults remember that temperament is also important and should not be overlooked. The judge must have a perception of faults and their seriousness. Common faults in the breed include: a small or apple shaped head; snipey muzzle and narrow jaws; flat or indistinct withers; soft topline; narrow chest and rear quarters; cow hocks; short stepping with a lack of reach and drive; fine bone and lacking substance; too short legs; soft and woolly (frizzy) coat;

Int. PL Ch Rendi Kontekst Nadwislan, European Winner '04 and Club Winner '01. A top size male - tolerance should always be given to dogs standing at the top and slightly over the standard, but **never** below it.

Int. PL Ch Wilga z Gangu Dlugich, Club Winner '99, with the shape I love to see! It is hard to find PONs with this shape in some countries. Photo: A Stepinski.

Judges should think about the breed's function. The PON is not a small dog, it is a much bigger dog than its body suggests at first view. It is a herder and a flock protector, hardy, weather resistant, intelligent, strong and muscular. The PON does not fly around the ring at great speed, he moves easily and with purpose. Not all breeds were developed to be fast moving dogs!

The breed standard has undergone few changes since the original composition of 1956 and probably needs no significant change in finite detail but rather more depth of understanding when it comes to interpreting it. Any changes recently proposed have been as the result of poor original translation from Polish to English and the number of misleading written publications that have been published. Therefore, I would urge anyone wishing to judge the PON to look at old pictures of the great dogs of the breed. Better feeding, grooming and coat care will lead to obvious changes but study the essential proportions of these dogs and develop an understanding of type. Understanding the history of the breed's development will help you to understand the essence of the breed.

Whilst many breeds (especially in the UK) bemoan the streamlining of their original standards to a more sterile modern version, the Polish breeders bemoan the insertion of additional text in to their standard, when no such similar words and phrases appeared in the Polish versions! Just one word can make a huge difference.

The FCI standard requires the breed to be compact, the AKC and KC chooses the word cobby - the two terms can be interpreted entirely differently. Cobby is often taken to mean square, compact to be well coupled and thick set. To avoid misinterpretation it would be preferable if all standards used the word 'compact' as this more adequately describes the PON's general appearance.

A dog show in Bytom, 1963

'Type' versus 'Movement'

Why is 'type' important? Because it is what makes a PON a PON and not a Tibetan Terrier! You must be clear in your own mind which virtues are directly related to type. You must decide what it is that renders a dog untypical. For me type is the first impression the dog gives. Type shouts "I am a PON" and linked to the PON's correct character and disposition adds "Look at me!"

Type is the combination of characteristics that makes the breed what it is - it is not just about anatomical construction, a perfectly constructed dog may lack breed type and vice versa. I can recall one successful PON that was a beautifully constructed dog but for me, it just wasn't a PON.

Type for me is a dog correctly proportioned, with a good medium sized head, good neck, distinct withers, strong, wide back and loin, angulated to move with efficient reach and drive, giving an impression of compactness and strength, with no exaggerations and covered with a long straight, weather proof coat. Width, strength, substance, compactness and robustness are all essentials of the breed and the dog must move with a gait that is typical for the breed, not one that looks spectacular to the ringside.

When judging I look for the most typical PON with the most typical, accurate movement. If all move equally well and are equally beautiful - which has the most style, which one makes you think "I want a PON like that in my kennel", which takes your breath away, has that stamp of quality and lots of expression, one will have it (hopefully). Eliminate on type and movement, if you can't do this, substance/body condition, muscle, general appearance and coat.

The type versus movement argument is a difficult one. The best moving PON may not be the most typical for the breed. Obviously you want a typical, sound dog, if you put sound movement up over better type eventually you will have good moving dogs that may not look like PONs anymore, conversely if you judge just to type you can have wonderful PONs that can't do an hour's work let alone a day. So you must compromise and look for the dog which has a better than average level of type and soundness.

Essential to the appearance and qualities of endurance in all dogs are the structural features that govern balance and the ability to move freely - angulation. A good herding dog has limbs that extend freely and the balance of body for trotting for many hours without tiring.

When assessing movement - remember that you are looking not just for physical soundness but for the PON's typical movement. Not all dogs are the same breed, not all breeds move in

The PON's general appearance is of a medium sized, shaggy sheepdog.

the same way or at the same speed. High kicking hocks, however spectacular, are untypical and more than likely due to an imbalance between front and hind angulation. Excessive angulation in any part of the body is detrimental to joint support and endurance.

At higher level competition, and especially at group level, are judges looking for the complete show dog, flashy and sound enough, but not exactly epitomizing its breed type? Is it more difficult for such judges to appreciate the 'stranger' breeds, those which are not glamorous but were just built for their working or utility purpose and may be superior examples? Do we, as breeders and judges, just want a sound, showy, charismatic dog regardless of the breed? Have you ever had a dog that to you has not epitomized breed type, that did not conform to your ideal of the breed standard but yet you found yourself looking at the dog and thinking "I can win with this dog"? Then you start to compromise your views and principles for the sake of the red rosette and the dog becomes a top winner and soon everyone else aspires to breed that type too. What then happens to breed type? What is the level of responsibility of the breeder in maintaining type and what is the level of responsibility of the judge?

The original functions of many of our breeds have become obsolete - and so it is for the PON as our societies have changed from agrarian into urban societies. By forgetting the breed's original form and function, even though the breed's modern role is very different, is to move away from true breed type.

The dog's movement is a measure of its conformation. To compromise and allow changes that may appeal to more all-round and group judges is to risk an alteration in the breed type. Understanding sound movement is important, understanding typical movement is essential to the preservation of breed type. Learning and quoting the breed standard is all well and good but means nothing if you do not understand what is behind the words - the breed's history, function and development. Learning and understanding are two different things.

Returning to Lehtinen and Lummelampi "a dog, however well muscled and however well moving, is not a typical example of its breed if it does not have typical movement. And if we accept small changes in the movement of a breed, we accept small changes in conformation, proportions and overall breed type until we end up with an identikit show dog."

'Balance' and 'Conditioning'

'Balance' is a very important aspect when evaluating the PON. Balance is dependent upon the proportion between the size of head, length of neck, depth of chest and length of legs and body, each to the other. Balance is also required between front and rear angulation to give the desired movement. Lack of structural balance is the reason for much incorrect movement. Balance is quite literally the perfect balance and correctness of all the component parts of the dog, each in harmony with the other.

According to Page Elliott, good angulation "facilitates a ground-covering stride. Balance facilitates good foot-timing. Joints that control movement should flex easily and smoothly, providing strong thrust from the rear with spring and resilience in the forehand. The swing and extension of the forelegs should coordinate with the action of the rear so that there will be no overstepping or interfering".

All show dogs need exercise and conditioning beyond a quick run around the garden or a few rounds around the ring to keep them in top form and peak condition, and to enable them to present their typical movement to advantage. The right exercise and proper muscle tone enhance good, typical movement. It takes many muscles, working together, to produce sound movement. In the front assembly, as there is no collar bone, muscular support alone helps stabilize the shoulders against the spine and chest well.

Good angulation gives wider spread to the muscles due to the fact that the shoulder bones and pelvis are properly slanted. A dog with upright structure in front and rear quarters will have poor general muscle tone and so move poorly.

With coated breeds, breeders and exhibitors often struggle to balance the show requirements of maintaining the coat in top condition with the requirement to maintain the dog underneath in peak physical condition with proper exercise. Judges usually look for both but it is a difficult balancing act. This is why you may find flabby dogs with flowing coats, or well-muscled dogs with broken coats - surely we should be looking for a happy medium. Whilst a long coat is desirable, a quality coat is more important if we consider the breed's function. A double layered, weatherproof coat will protect the PON irrespective of whether it is 10cms or 20cms long; a soft or thin coat will not. It is possible to have a PON with a correct and long coat who is freely exercised and still 'glamorous' enough for the ring.

DANGERS TO THE BREED

The view coming from Poland is that there is a potential danger that some countries will develop a type of PON that is different to the type the Poles require - "It is not good when PONs are bred smaller than the standard and PONs especially are being bred below the standard in some countries that love a smaller, delicate type build. This is not good. We should protect our PON from these tendencies and preserve the type we recommend…"

I have had a few critics over the years for expressing this same feeling about the breed's development in the UK and this comment,

PONs enjoy the mental stimulation of a varied exercise routine. Show dogs have lives too! Pictured here are Multi Ch Pompon z Wielgowa, Sasquehanna Szymon and Int.PL Ch Eter z Banciarni.

from the proposed commentary, is directed largely at the UK. I think that too many judges (and breeders) think that a male over 18.5 inches or a bitch over 17.5/18ins is too big and are promoting males at 17 ins and bitches at 16ins and even under the standard.

I believe that the major issues for the future are the lack of size and substance; short legged dogs; domed heads with extremely short muzzles probably 0.5:1, small eyes and very deep stops - this alters the whole expression of the PON and is an uncharacteristic head; no, or flat, withers producing an incorrect outline and short stepping, restricted movement.

I worry about the general trend toward a lack of size, substance and compactness. Type, soundness and overall balance have to be highly important but it must be Polish type. I would hate to see a

Int.PL Ch Lopuch Baltycka Rapsodia by Dymek Gapcio Baltycka Rapsodia ex Nocka Baltycka Rapsodia. Breeder/owner Anna Zakrzewska.

PL Ch Kaduk z Ogrodka Magdy by Ch Cis spod Winnego Krzewu ex Ch Agusia z Nadwarcianskiej Doliny. Breeder Tadeusz Zelazny.

1991 Club Winner, World Winner Ch Bartnik z Matecznika Diany by Ch Radosz z Psiego Raju ex Ch Brussa z Doliny Biebrzy

divergence in type to an English Lowland Sheepdog and a Polish Lowland Sheepdog and the breed to go down the route of the German Shepherd Dog.

5. Breeding and Choosing Your Puppy

Much can be said about the subject of breeding but I do not intend to give a practical guide on how to achieve a successful mating, how to care for the pregnant bitch or the practicalities of whelping and rearing a litter. There are plenty of other good books available that will take you through the process. However, often, not enough is said about the planning that should go in to any prospective litter and I think two questions need to be considered - 'what is my goal in breeding in a litter?' and 'what are my reasons for choosing which dogs to use for breeding?'

Today's breeders are entirely responsible for tomorrow's PONs and this responsibility should not be taken lightly. What's more, after your puppies have gone to their new homes they remain your responsibility for the rest of their lives.

Breeders have a responsibility to ensure that they only try to promote correct type, soundness and temperament. As far as possible only the best and fittest (both physically and mentally) are bred from and that the health of the breed is maintained. In addition, puppies should be suitably raised, properly socialized and placed in stable homes.

Before going ahead with breeding plans, breeders need to make some personal and professional decisions. Most breeders' goals will be to breed healthy, family dogs that may have some show potential.

Anyone buying such a dog should expect to get a healthy dog (and a healthy dog is surely a reasonable expectation?) Breeders should know about any genetic disease in their breed, be able to discuss genetic disease in a reasonable manner and identify any of their dogs with genetic defects.

A well balanced puppy will stand four-square and a well constructed puppy will stride out showing good driving action.

A good breeder aims to produce sound, healthy, functional dogs that approximate to the ideal. A good breeding programme is all about selecting the best and mating the best to the best, not to the most convenient. To try to produce the ideal, then the breeder must know what the ideal is. It often happens that you can try your hardest to breed the best you have to the best you can and often end up disappointed. There are no guarantees.

Everyone's goal should be to strive to breed better and better PONs that would not look out of place in the homeland. You can never stop learning - study pedigrees, learn about genetics, talk with respected breeders in Poland, set yourself goals and try to breed as closely to the standard as you can. Always try to learn and improve your understanding of the breed. Breed for breed type, genetic integrity, good temperament and structural soundness.

Selecting the Sire and Dam

When selecting the right sire, always begin by knowing the strengths and weaknesses of the bitch you hope to breed from. If you don't know her good and bad points then any dog will do! Your goal should be to focus on the specific traits of conformation, health and temperament. Studying pedigrees can help a breeder learn about the qualities and lack of qualities in the bitch and in any potential sires. Successful breeding is about being able to distinguish between ordinary dogs and outstanding ones.

There is no direct way of looking into a pedigree to see if the desired or undesired genes are present and so an indirect method is needed. This means finding out about the phenotypes of the ancestors for three generations and learning about the littermates of the bitch and each potential sire you are considering. The former approach is called pedigree depth and the latter breadth of pedigree. Both are useful methods.

Not all show quality dogs should be bred from. Some may not have the temperament for it! A good stud dog or brood bitch reproduces themselves and adds more to the breed. Some may not do this and produce mixed quality and type in their progeny.

As Dr Malcolm Willis says "You've always got to try to select stock that is not only much better than the breed average, but much better than your kennel average. If you breed from parents that are better than average, their progeny will be better than average, but not, on average, as good as their parents. If you breed from parents that are worse than average, their progeny will also be worse than average, but not, on average, as poor as the parents. There is, in effect, a pull to the mean. And that's why it can be so hard to improve a breed".

Ch Apasz z Bankowcow, Club Winner '84.
Seven of his daughters became Polish champions.

Int. PL.CS Ch Czekan Moscic, sire of 24 champions. Breeder/owner Regina Szyszkowska.

Cost, convenience and show results are often considered as legitimate reasons when choosing a stud dog but they actually have nothing to do with the genetics of the dog or what is heritable. The best reasons should always include the core factors: conformation, health, history, temperament and the qualities seen in the offspring.

However, this is not always the case - the five most popular reasons for selecting a stud dog are:

1. Convenience - proximity to the residence of the bitch
2. Cost - the cheapest stud dog!
3. Pedigree - a number of champion ancestors
4. Offspring - produced were quality pups
5. Ancestors/littermates - known producers

In her work on top producing dams and sires in Poland, Anna Dominiak has started a valuable database on those dogs who have had the most influence on the Polish PON population, using the number of Polish champion or junior champion progeny to rank them. The list contains 44 sires and 40 dams.

Many of those listed appear in pedigrees worldwide and this is a useful information point for breeders. Pedigree charts trace the sire bloodlines from Szlem z Babiej Wsi and Smok z Kordegardy and the dam bloodlines from Bajda z Babiej Wsi, Certa z Melna, Arabella z Alty and Ustka z Kordegardy. You can find more information on these dogs in Chapter 9.

CHOOSING YOUR PUPPY

Experience is a good teacher because you learn from your mistakes. Breeders who learn as they go, learn what to look out for. Often many puppies are selected based on their expression, personality, colour, coat texture or size. Each of these traits gives them a special appeal but these traits alone are not enough. Breeders and buyers need to consider health, temperament and conformation as a package in choosing their pups. We are possibly all guilty of keeping puppies we should never have kept and regretting letting others go, later in life.

You have to distinguish between the pick of the litter and the best breeding material. Many breeders are quite capable of deciding which puppy is the best in the litter but given some experience of the breed and bloodlines, the pick of the litter is not so difficult to find. The difficulty lies in deciding whether the pick of the litter is an outstanding dog in breed terms. Puppies should be evaluated for breed type and structural soundness equally and in relation to the standard and not to each other. Puppies should be evaluated for structural soundness one at a time and preferably not by the breeder as personal preferences may creep in and the evaluation will no longer be objective.

Different breeders will have different ideas on when and how to evaluate their puppies. I evaluate my puppies at roughly 8 weeks. Bones grow at different rates so it is important to realise that the proportion of bone growth is as similar to the adult structure at 8 weeks as it is ever going to be during the growth of the puppy. Basically this means that what you see at 8 weeks is what you will get later in life. You should evaluate the whole litter but not against each other, but against a structured and objective grading system that will help you maintain a focus on breeding type and overall quality. Subjective grading encourages you to look at the whole dog and not to overlook weaknesses in favour of the puppy that captures your heart.

If you want to be a top breeder then trying to represent a mediocre dog as great is self defeating therefore you must be honest and not keep or breed from any dog that doesn't measure up to at least average in your grading system. You should only be looking to keep dogs which are an improvement in type and structural quality over what you already have.

Whilst it is ideal to evaluate the puppies only at 8 weeks it is virtually impossible to stop yourself from evaluating (or forming some general ideas) about your puppies from the moment they are born, let alone from the first day they get to their feet or the first day they break in to a trot. It's just human nature. However, I do believe that what you see at 8 weeks is what the puppy will most likely grow into as an adult dog.

So what do you look for at 8 weeks? The four most important things must be: temperament, overall balance, proportions (in relation to the breed standard) and the whole picture. There are many theories for evaluating temperament. I like to pick the puppy up and cradle it in my arms, on its back. An insecure puppy will hold onto your arms with its front paws; with a fearful puppy you can see the fear in the whites of its eyes - this puppy will need a lot of socialization.

An aggressive puppy will not let you hold it on its back and the puppy that avoids eye contact with you will not bond so well with humans later in life. A good genetic temperament means that the puppy will be calm and relaxed in this position and confident that

Sasquehanna Kubrak Ponadto at 10 weeks and seven months.
Breeder Malgorzata Supronowicz.

nothing will happen to them. With PONs there is no significant difference between the temperament of the male and the female.

Temperaments can vary and you cannot define a 'normal' temperament. Insecurity and aggression do not tend to be problem in the breed, however the PON can be a quite dominant breed. You can also observe temperament in the puppy's reaction to its surroundings and when introduced into strange surroundings. The puppy's personality should match the personality and fit with the lifestyle of the prospective owner.

If you hold the puppy in a suspended position in the air so it is bearing no weight and is relaxed, then a well structured puppy will hang in a very nearly stacked position. I think you should be looking for a strong, compact (but not square), stocky, wide puppy. You do not want a narrow puppy at 8 weeks as this is what you'll get later in life.

In PONs you want a wide breast, wide back and wide loin and when you pick the puppy up it should feel heavy, not delicate or fragile. His head and muzzle should also be wide with solid pigment on his nose, eyes and lips. By feeling the cheek bones and zygomatic arch you can make a judgement on whether the head will grow on in proportion or not. If you draw a line along the topline and the head is not well above that line then the puppy has a short neck. All dogs have 7 vertebrae in the neck and a poorly placed front assembly or straight shoulder will produce a shortened neck. His eyes should be bright and clear and his expression lively; check for a scissor bite and good occlusion (bite) of the side teeth.

At 8 weeks the depth of the chest should be to the elbow and if the bottom of the chest feels flat, the puppy should retain that depth. The length of the loin is measured from the last rib off the spine to the pelvis. If the loin is too long you may have topline problems, if the loin is too short then the dog will have reduced flexibility to turn and twist. If you drop an imaginary plumb line from the point of buttock to the ground, with a well balanced and well structured rear assembly, the line would drop to the edge of the toes.

To check the placement of the feet, pick up the rear slightly and drop it. Hocks should be perpendicular to the ground and the hock joint should have no forward (slipped or double jointed) or sideward motion. The topline should be broad, level and strong. Topline problems rarely come from the spine but usually relate to problems with the front or rear assembly. A soft, dipping, weak or roached topline is usually because the back is compensating for a weakness elsewhere.

When put on the ground or moved outside of the bed, the PON puppy should be curious about its surroundings, eager to explore and happy to play. Sometimes it is difficult to get them to stand on a table or any other surface in a good show position and stacking him at this age could mislead your decisions. When standing the puppy you should stand him in the most natural position rather than trying to 'fix him'. It is much better to assess movement and balance with the puppy allowed to move freely. See how he moves in profile and straight up and down - are his legs moving with a free parallel action? When he comes to a natural stop does he stand himself four-square in a balanced way? A puppy that constantly moves one rear leg forward may have a weakness in the hock.

To be comfortable standing still then the puppy must be well made and balanced. When you watch the puppies moving naturally on the ground you can see their attitude and how they carry themselves. The best built, best balanced puppies usually trot freely, those that 'bunny hop' may not be so well built and balanced.

Substance and size means very little at 8 weeks; the smallest puppy may turn out to be the biggest adult and vice versa. However the puppy should feel the right weight and its weight should be in balance with the whole puppy.

At this age, the puppy's coat will be comparatively short but it should be thick and plush. Colour and markings are purely about personal choice as all colours and markings are acceptable. A genetic colour pattern is not definitely established in the breed. Most PONs carry a dominant 'fading' factor genetically, which means that puppies are born darker in coat colour than they will appear as adults. Coats will begin to lighten by 12 weeks, with changes first becoming noticeable at the roots of the outer coat. The coat colour will reach its lightest stage at 12 to 18 months then darken as the dog matures.

The intensity of coat colour can change many times during the dog's life but they will never return to the colour of their birth coat. Some, albeit a few, remain black and white or black into adulthood.

The breed standard calls for a medium sized, unexaggerated dog, which means that there should be balance between the set (angulation) of the bones and muscle mass. Bones and muscles must be balanced to work in unsion.

The PON is not a dog of extremes.

6. Living with PONs

The PON is not the breed for everyone. Do not be fooled by their medium size, cute exterior and fun characters. This is a strong willed, stubborn breed, which can be very independent. It is not unusual to find breeders, exhibitors and pet owners who have enjoyed the company of Bearded Collies and Bobtails, look to the PON for a smaller (and they think more manageable) version of their larger sheepdog and then be surprised to find what a handful they can be. I spent the first 16 years of my life living with OES and they are a lovely breed but when compared to the PON they are totally different. A Bobtail will do anything to please you, a PON will please itself and think about you later, usually if there's a reward in it for him. The PON is far superior in intelligence to the Bobtail and will dominate them and literally run circles around them.

The PON is a family dog, if you do not wish to live with your dogs, a PON is not the breed for you.

TEMPERAMENT AND BEHAVIOUR

The PON is lively, curious, aloof and very territorial. From day one you must establish a firm but kind relationship with them and form a mutual respect. The PON will quickly take advantage if you are inconsistent in your commands and can be quite defiant. If the PON doesn't recognize you as pack leader (and they are very quick to establish pack hierarchy) then you may find that it is the PON who leads you. This in turn can lead to problems such as independence during exercise, a disregard for commands, a dog which behaves in a dominant, protective way with you when he feels you are threatened by other people or dogs and even to fighting for dominance. Even if you are 'leader', you will still find occasions when the PON will decide he is not going to listen to you.

I find their behaviour very different on a one-to-one basis to in a pack. When you own more than one PON, the pack behaviour is very strong and so is their independence of mind, if the moment suits them. They have a unique knack of 'going deaf' and as they disappear over the hills in front of you don't bother shouting 'come back' but instead shout 'when are you coming back?'! That is not to say they cannot be trained because they can and they learn very quickly - both good and bad habits - and as long as you reward them with food, they are happy to learn.

If the PON wants something - he barks. Remember these were dogs that were capable of hunting wild boar and were 'guarders'. The PON did not work blindly to commands, but often on his own, thinking for himself not listening for the whistles of the shepherd. Whilst he worked, he barked!

The PON will often give the appearance of being quite aggressive as he will bark furiously at strangers, but true to the saying, his bark is far worse than his bite. He is also often somewhat reserved when it comes to unfamiliar people, but this is typical of a sheepdog. It does not mean that the dog is afraid or insecure because he will still look straight at you even if he is backing away. At the same time as being reserved, he is also interested and curious. The PON still has a strong herding instinct and a very good nose for tracking. He is a reliable watchdog with natural sharpness. In the house he has a quiet temperament.

This is a breed that is easily bored and when the PON gets bored he finds his own entertainment - chewing, digging, beheading flowers - frequently owners say that their PON is a 'very good gardener'. Raiding the rubbish bins is another favourite pastime - they are greedy, they have a natural instinct to find their own food and they will usually eat anything - living, dead or decaying. This must be a natural habit from their time as farm dogs, living off scraps and finding their own food and water when necessary.

They do not do well in situations where they are left alone for long periods of time and like nothing better than to be close to their family. The PON will often seek out the cooler places to lie, tiled and wooden floors are often preferable to carpet and they cope very well with extremes of heat and cold.

The PON is very adaptable to his living space and is an excellent companion for children; he will protect and watch them as well as his home. The breed is good natured and gentle with children.

The PON is a breed which is very loyal, faithful and great fun, as they love to play, but demand a firm but gentle owner; they are not submissive lapdogs, they are not mindless followers but they are great companions and a fun and loyal 'buddy' for children.

TRAINING AND SOCIALISATION

Spending quality time training your PON will pay huge rewards later. As with most breeds, it is important to put great emphasis on the process of establishing yourself as leader and thereby removing the dog from any stressful situations when it thinks it must be the leader and decision maker. Whilst this obviously applies in all human-canine relationships, I think it is so important when the canine in question is a PON.

It is important that the PON is given quality training time, quality play time and allowed to spend quality time with his human family.

If you are intending to show then you must teach the dog to stand as well as the usual sit, stay and down commands. The PONs, with their love of food, are very easy to 'bait' in the ring but don't allow them to be so obsessed with the treat that the judge finds it

PONs are great family dogs with a playful sense of humour.

impossible to attract their attention when required or they become too excited and no longer listen to you.

PONs mature mentally and physically quite early in life, so training at a young age is essential. A good and consistent training programme will go a long way to establishing desirable behaviour later in life. A one year old PON is nearly fully developed even though he may still act like a puppy.

Many of the habits and behaviour - good and bad - that has been learnt and exhibited when a puppy, will be retained for a very long time. I have an old male, who when excited or about to go for a walk, will gently grab and mouth my hand or tug my sleeve and bite his collar and lead, leading to a tug of war session and making it generally difficult to get it over his head. This is my fault as I allowed him to do this as an adorable 4 month old puppy; at nearly eleven he is still doing it and I'm sure always will.

7. Caring for Your PON

FEEDING AND NUTRITION

Years of utility usefulness, harsh conditions and the ability to find its own food means that the PON is a good eater and also uses every nutritional element of his meal very well. As a farm dog in Poland, he was used to working at his best with very little food, so he must be fed accordingly. As with any dog, a proper diet is essential for fitness and health, but the dog's diet must be tailored to suit the individual and its lifestyle. PONs have always been hardworking dogs that thrived on a limited diet. This diet may have consisted of bread, potatoes, vegetables such as cabbage, cottage cheese and sometimes even an egg.

The PON is not a fussy eater and will eat as much food as you offer him. However the PON's metabolism does not always suit the modern, commercial foods. They have a slow metabolism and do not require high levels of protein and fat, just the right amount of protein of good biological value and enough fibre, vitamins and minerals.

Excess protein in the PON's diet seems to lead to skin problems and obesity. In adulthood, if feeding a commercial 'complete' food, I always look to feed on or below 25% protein. Obviously it is different for puppies because of development and growth, however a too-protein rich diet can also lead to scratching, itching and rapid growth spurts at a young age. Excessive levels of nutrients can be as damaging as insufficient levels so I feed my dogs a balanced mix of commercial food plus vegetables, rice, egg and some fresh meat. Many breeders have moved to the natural BARF (Bones and Raw Food) diet and reported excellent results. There are a number of useful websites dedicated to BARF diets and particularly regarding this diet and the PON.

Obesity comes down to either too little exercise or too many calories and again, you must find the balance. As with humans, it is far easier to put weight on than it is to get it off! Maintaining a PON in optimum condition is a skill that breeders and exhibitors need to learn. By allowing your PON to become overweight you risk shortening his lifespan - a fat PON is a lazy PON!

Whilst many books focus on correct feeding, very few talk about the care of teeth, something that is equally important for the pet and show dog alike.

Preserving the PON Smile

One of the PON's most endearing traits is that he has the capability to 'smile'. This is great sight to behold when he greets your return, or waits excitedly to have his lead put on to go out. You also see it when you're cross and telling him off - he'll say sorry with smile!

Domestication of the dog resulted in his food being presented to him, he no longer had to hunt and kill his dinner. Over the years, the dog foods available have become highly sophisticated, designed to satisfy every nutritional need.

A simple survey of the bewildering choices of foods available at the supermarket revealed an alarming discovery. Most tinned food and some dried foods contained 'various sugars', some were 'coloured with caramel' - Sugar!

If you consider the nutritional needs of your dog (and even yourself) you need protein, carbohydrate and even fat, etc. to survive, but what you do not need in any shape or form is sugar. All mouths contain bacteria, they are meant to co-exist with their host, which they do, until sugar is introduced into the mouth. These bugs then spring into action and metabolise the sugar into acid. Therefore, the more often you give the dog something containing

The typical PON smile - don't confuse it for aggression!

sugar, the more often his teeth will be bathed in acid. Acid demineralises the surface covering the tooth - the enamel - and leads to tooth decay. Some breeders in Poland give old bread, baked in the oven until hard or carrots to help clean teeth. Special teeth cleaning chews, toys, toothbrushes and toothpaste are also very useful.

EXERCISE

The PON is fairly adaptable; if you want him to do a two mile walk he will, if you can only manage twenty minutes playing ball in the garden then he'll also be happy with that, but this is a working breed and good musculature is important for physical fitness and protection against injury. I feel it is important that the PON is allowed time for free running everyday. Of course, care must be taken not to over exercise youngsters or to allow them to run madly, jump and twist in a way that may cause injury and lead to future structural damage.

The PON has a natural curiosity, which in turn leads to paddling in streams, putting heads in to holes, venturing into thick undergrowth and generally exploring their surroundings to the full. I feel firmly that PONs which are 'show dogs' are first and foremost dogs and should be allowed the pleasures of free exercise and the mental stimulation it gives.

THE AGEING PON

A new formula for working out the dog's age in relation to a human's has been developed, which is based on new information and a better understanding of the aging process. This suggests that the old formula was not correct because it assumed that each year of life was linear, meaning that it was exactly the same year after year. With a new understanding of how time passes and with some knowledge about how each species develops and matures, it is now believed that the aging process does not continue at the same pace year after year.

All species do not grow, develop, and mature at the same rate. In the table overpage, the old and new formulae show the conversion of a dog's age into man-years.

What has not changed between the old and new formulae is the first year of life; it is still the equivalent of 15 or 16 man-years. But after that things begin to change, A two-year-old dog would be equivalent to a 24 year-old man; a three year-old dog would be equivalent to a 28year-old and so on.

CANINE AGE CONVERTED TO MAN-YEARS

Chronological Age	1	2	3	4	5	6	7	8
Old Formula	15	7	7	7	7	7	7	7
New Formula	16	8	4	4	4	4	4	4

The reason for the change in the old formula is because it is believed that the aging process is affected by many factors, not just the clock and the calendar. For example, diet, rest and health care for the younger members of a species are clearly different than those of the adults. How well these elements are managed plays a major role in the extension of their biological clock and their life expectancy.

PONs have a good lifespan; a generally fit and active PON should live to around 12 years of age, many live longer, even to 16. A PON is considered old at about 8 years of age and very old at 12 years of age. PONs age gracefully without any major health changes as they advance to old age. However their needs do change - they need more sleep, more opportunity to go to the toilet, their senses, speed and alertness decrease and they need more rest, comfort and love.

Older dogs need a regular, daily routine and careful observation. The teeth, heart, lungs, eyes and ears may slowly and gradually deteriorate and owners should be aware of lumps or tumours under the skin. Nutritionally the PON's requirements alter and he needs smaller, perhaps more frequent meals, of a high biological value but with less minerals.

Most PONs age without personality changes so it pays to be observant to any small physical or behavioural changes that may be early warning signs that future veterinary help may be needed.

Above:
Cwik spod Zagla, Garda Wtora z Kordegardy, Cuma spod Zagla, Dux spod Zagla, Dar spod Zagla

Left: Kontrapunkt Lawenda and Lubianka z Kordegardy

Right: Gaja ze Starego Lupkowa, Wacpan z Kordegardy and Marzanna z Kordegedary

Left: Cuma spod Zagla and Doman z Kordegardy

8. Grooming and coat care

The PON is a double coated breed. This means that he has a soft, thick undercoat and hard outer coat. Professor Wieslaw Szczepanski from the University in Olsztyn has undertaken some preliminary research in to the structure of the breed's coat and these initial investigations form part of an ongoing research project. A relatively small number of samples have been examined but it appears that the males overall grow thicker and longer coats than the bitches. The long top coat was thicker in bitches than in males, but with males, the undercoat was thicker and longer.

The general colour/markings of the dog had an affect on the coat. From the small amount of samples analysed to date it appears that parti colours have a shorter and thicker coat than solid coloured dogs. No conclusions have yet been drawn on any differences between the different colour coats of the solid dogs, ie between solid blacks and solid greys etc.

The PON's coat serves to protect him from extremes of heat and cold and should be weatherproof. A PON with a correct and good quality coat will take a long time to get wet to the skin when you are bathing him. Judging the dogs in wet weather quickly shows up those with correct coats and those that are just 'fluffballs'! If the PON has the required harsh coat then it is not difficult to look after him. Grooming every ten days or so will keep him clean - even without a bath! Males will benefit from having their stomachs washed every now and then to clean the coat of urine stains and smells. The hair which grows in the ear canal should be plucked regularly to allow the free flow of air and the hair on the pads trimmed. Otherwise, the coat is best kept as natural as possible.

With pets and older dogs, if you clip off the coat to the skin, thereby removing the undercoat, you expose the dog to the elements. It is a myth that the PON will be cooler if he is clipped to the skin, quite the contrary, by removing the undercoat the sun now has direct access to the skin and the PON will be far hotter than if he was still wearing his coat. After clipping it is not unusual for the coat to grow back softer and less coarse than before.

Another myth is that cutting the hair from the fall will help them to see better. The PON's hair characteristically falls over his eyes and this serves two purposes: when the PON was working it would have protected him from the dust of the hoofs of any stock and it also serves to polarize the light, giving the PON better vision. Cutting it off, brushing it back or tieing it up does the dog no favours. If you do tie it up, leave some strands of hair still falling over the eyes.

An ungroomed, unmanaged coat will mat easily. Mats quickly form over small, foreign bodies like twigs, grass, thorns and seeds, and are often found at the base of ears, under the armpits and chin and on the belly or between the rear legs. The dog will find these mats uncomfortable, even painful, if left in the coat for long periods of time.

A correctly exercised dog should not require any nail clipping as the nails will naturally be kept down to the right length, however, it may depend on the type of surface the dogs are being exercised on. Owners of PON's with tails need to be vigilant for soiling underneath the tail and the male dog may require some tidying up around the sheath.

Although it is clearly stated in the standard that the PON should be presented naturally without any scissoring, natural presentation does not meaning looking as if the dog has just come off a farm; but over grooming is, in my view, as bad.

The dog should be clean, free from mats and presented in a natural way, as a shaggy sheepdog.

Different dogs have different coat textures and different behavioral patterns. If your dog is trained to lie quietly on his side while you groom it makes grooming easier, so start them off young. I always brush all my puppies from 4 weeks and upwards and bath and blow dry everyone before they go to new homes.

Grooming can be very therapeutic for dog and owner and often the dogs enjoy the attention. It is not unusual once you have finished grooming one dog for another to come and try to get on the table or sit in your lap for some attention.

Show Grooming

Everyone has their own techniques, favoured tools and tried and trusted 'trade secrets'. Having been brought up with Old English Sheepdogs I think I know most of the 'tricks' and have always found the PON's coat more than manageable. The harsher and more correct the coat is, the easier it will be to groom. I believe in the saying that 'you bath a coat in and you bath a coat out' and often prefer to groom my PONs wet, either after bathing and whilst being dried or by using a water spray.

I always wash them before a show, unless the show falls on consecutive weekends and then it is just a 'top and tail job' - faces, rear ends and legs.

If your PON has the correct coat then bathing a few days before a show will not ruin it. One of my dogs was often washed the day before a show as I like to see white dogs, white. It was never a problem. Use a good quality shampoo with no added oils and it will be fine; the many 'harsh coat' shampoos are also a good option.

Soft coats will still be soft whether you have washed them or not. A dirty coat feels very different to a naturally harsh coat!

Faces and feet often stain and may require additional help to get back to their natural colour. Lemon juice and cornflour makes an excellent (and natural) whitening paste for stubborn stains.

Int.PL Ch Dlaczego z Gangu Dlugich, a daughter of Zacierka. Whether you show or not your PON needs regular grooming to keep him mat free.
Photo Hartley.

A practical 'teddy-bear' haircut.

When presented in the ring the fall should not be brushed back nor should the topline be parted, the PON should not be presented like a Bearded Collie. The standard calls for natural presentation and no scissoring but I am not adverse to tidying up around the feet and rear end a little.

Pet Grooming

Part of the beauty of the breed is its coat and many prospective pet owners are first attracted to the shaggy look of the dog. I always think it's a shame to then clip off the dog but a nice 'teddy bear' or poodle cut of a few inches all over is often more manageable for the pet owner and also more comfortable for the ageing PON. This doesn't mean that they require no further grooming. Hopefully much of the undercoat is left intact, if a little thinned and the top coat length trimmed back. This PON will still require a regular brush through to keep the undercoat mat free. If the coat is clipped correctly it will grow out evenly.

It is the responsibility of the breeder to make sure that any new or prospective owners know what to expect in terms of coat management, understand coat changes, are shown the correct brushes and combs, are made aware of problem areas such as ears and elbows and understand that the dog also has hairy inner pads and hairy inner ears. These need regular checking and trimming or plucking.

9. PONs of influence

There are many PONs that have influenced the breed since the post war years, some as showdogs, some as sires and dams, others as international and national ambassadors for the PON. Over the years my knowledge of, and opinions about, the breed and what I look for both in terms of structural conformation, type and temperament have been hugely influenced by studying pedigrees, talking with Polish breeders and meeting, first hand, some outstanding PONs.

This chapter presents some of those PONs who have had a strong influence on the breed through the years. A useful reference guide for any dedicated breed enthusiast and an excellent book for appreciating many of the great Polish champions is Barbara Larska's *Ksiega Championow 2000* (Polish champions from the first to hold the title - Amok Moniek - to the year 2000. It also includes junior champions).

Barbara Larska presented some of the most important breeding lines for the Lodz Congress 2003. The purpose of her report was to map the development of the Polish Lowland Sheepdog in its country of origin. The lines of sires and dams, including almost all the dogs used for breeding in the post-war restoration of the PON, were presented as line graphs. The study does not give information about the degree of the breeding relationship because the origin of the dam in the sire lines and paternity in the dam lines were not taken into consideration. Many breeders and enthusiasts worldwide may not be aware of the existence of this report nor had sight of a copy. For this reason the main body and context of Barbara's report is featured here.

Two dogs: Smok z Kordegardy (1949) and Szlem z Babiej Wsi (1949) and one bitch: Bajda z Babiej Wsi (1948) were the foundation for the breed's restoration. The whole PON population worldwide is based on these three lines. The participation of two further dams: Misia (1961) and Beta (1975) in the evolution of PON breeding lines remains insignificant.

Significant younger sires and dams were not considered because the report's context was to describe the most remarkable and meritorious dogs, no longer alive in the gene pool.

The line of Smok-Inkluz z Kordegardy has become less important in Polish PON breeding. Inkluz z Kordegardy, whose 10 descendants all won their Polish Championship, is present in pedigrees via his son Amok-Moniek, the first international champion and via his grandson Pasterz Bonus Pastor. Inkluz became well known outside of the Polish borders thanks to his great-grandson Ch. Zuk Urania, who was used at Lucienne Jasica's 'van het Goralenhof' kennel.

The most important descendant of Smok was his son Doman. This beautiful male produced numerous fabulous offspring including nine Champions. Two sons, Rumcajs and Rubin z Jurty, began two separate lines. Another son, Ch. Wigor-Gol z Jurty, also warrants mention here. He was the dog which was considered to be the typical representative of the breed - a strong boned male with a perfect head, beautiful top line, great coat and excellent movement. He was presented as the ideal PON at the 1st PON Club Dog Show in 1975. Unfortunately Wigor didn't produce any offspring and perhaps it can be assumed that this was caused by the inbreeding.

Rumcajs z Jurty was the father of the great, Polish and Danish Champion Zupan z Kordegardy. Although Zupan stayed in Poland for just a short period of time, he sired a remarkable son, Ch. Supel Filipon and left two grandsons: Ch. Lopuch Baltycka Rapsodia and Ch. Wiwat Pacynka. Rubin z Jurty, through his son Ch Cis spod Winnego Krzewu, was the grandsire of Ch. Kaduk z Ogrodka Magdy; Kaduk's grandson Ch. Iwan z Banciarni should also be mentioned here.

The next individual male deserving of more attention is Doman's grandson - Ch. Grog spod Zagla. His line did not evolve

Int.PL.CS Ch Amal z Banciarni, European Winner '90, Club winner '93 by Bart Agajax ex Turnia z Szalasu Puchatkow. Breeder Barbara Rayska-Swist. Photo at age $14^{1}/_{2}$.

Int.PL.Fin Ch Premier Oligarchia, Club Winner '96, World Winner '96, by Kusy Kawalkada ex Wena Pacynka Oligarchia. Breeder/owner Andrzej Stepinski.

Significant younger sires and dams were not considered because the report's context was to describe the most remarkable and meritorious dogs, no longer alive in the gene pool.

The line of Smok-Inkluz z Kordegardy has become less important in Polish PON breeding. Inkluz z Kordegardy, whose 10 descendants all won their Polish Championship, is present in pedigrees via his son Amok-Moniek, the first international champion and via his grandson Pasterz Bonus Pastor. Inkluz became well known outside of the Polish borders thanks to his great-grandson Ch. Zuk Urania, who was used at Lucienne Jasica's 'van het Goralenhof' kennel.

The most important descendant of Smok was his son Doman. This beautiful male produced numerous fabulous offspring including nine Champions. Two sons, Rumcajs and Rubin z Jurty, began two separate lines. Another son, Ch. Wigor-Gol z Jurty, also warrants mention here. He was the dog which was considered to be the typical representative of the breed - a strong boned male with a perfect head, beautiful top line, great coat and excellent movement. He was presented as the ideal PON at the 1st PON Club Dog Show in 1975. Unfortunately Wigor didn't produce any offspring and perhaps it can be assumed that this was caused by the inbreeding.

Rumcajs z Jurty was the father of the great, Polish and Danish Champion Zupan z Kordegardy. Although Zupan stayed in Poland for just a short period of time, he sired a remarkable son, Ch. Supel Filipon and left two grandsons: Ch. Lopuch Baltycka Rapsodia and Ch. Wiwat Pacynka. Rubin z Jurty, through his son Ch Cis spod Winnego Krzewu, was the grandsire of Ch. Kaduk z Ogrodka Magdy; Kaduk's grandson Ch. Iwan z Banciarni should also be mentioned here.

The next individual male deserving of more attention is Doman's grandson - Ch. Grog spod Zagla. His line did not evolve

Int.PL.CS Ch Amal z Banciarni, European Winner '90, Club winner '93 by Bart Agajax ex Turnia z Szalasu Puchatkow. Breeder Barbara Rayska-Swist. Photo at age $14^{1}/_{2}$.

Int.PL.Fin Ch Premier Oligarchia, Club Winner '96, World Winner '96, by Kusy Kawalkada ex Wena Pacynka Oligarchia. Breeder/owner Andrzej Stepinski.

quickly and only since the 90's and thanks to PON Club Winner'93 Ch. Amal z Banciarni has it become more significant.

Amal sired 13 Polish Champions and his son Ch. Furman Konkury won BOB at Westminster 2002, USA, when the breed was first shown with classes.

The Szlem z Babiej Wsi line developed very slowly and in the late 80's the Zeriba kennel finally used Jurand Grenada for breeding. He was the son of Ch. Witez z Kordegardy and produced many great sons with the 'z Zeriby' kennel name. Ch. Igor z Zeriby and Club Winner'84 - Ch. Apasz z Bankowcow were among them. Both sires contributed significantly to the breed, giving numerous outstanding offspring.

The line of Jurand - Apasz is behind Lar Rawipon and his son Ch. Maestro Misiura. Fortunately this branch evolved slowly and resulted in numerous female offspring; seven of Apasz z Bankowcow's daughters became Polish Champions.

The greatest role in Igor z Zeriby's line was played by Ch.Czekan Moscic. He gave a well developed sire line, produced 24 Polish Champions among his offspring and by became the top male in the table of 'Sires of Champions'.

The second son of Witez, Club Winner'75, Ch. Gwarek z Psiego Raju produced 4 champions. The unforgettable Ch. Radosz z Psiego Raju and his descendants are foremost amongst the many offspring of Gwarek. In this line are some very important sires such as: Club Winner'87, Ch. Palasz z Wielgowa and his grandson - Ch. Rokosz z Gangu Dlugich; the brothers: Ch. Bartosz Boruta and World and Club Winner' 91 Bartnik z Matecznika Diany with his son, Club Winner'95, Ch. Eter z Banciarni; and the father of 11 Polish Champions - World and Club Winner'96, Ch. Premier Oligarchia.

There are four main female lines. These are Bajda z Babiej Wsi (1948), Misia (1961), Beta (1975) and Wiga (1954). By far the most important female line comes from Bajda z Babiej Wsi; Misia's line can be considered almost dead, the other two represent around 5% of breeding lines.

Bajda gave birth to two daughters: Erga and Diuna z Babiej Wsi. The influencial dams coming from them were the foundation for new future lines. Certa z Melna comes from these lines and from her lines Arabella z Alty turned out to be the most important for Polish breeding. From Certa's direct line, Zoska z Kordegardy became the foundation dam for a German PON kennel and Forga z Kordegardy was the foundation for a kennel in Belgium. Arabella z Alty lived at the 'Urania' kennel and gave birth to Zenia, Watra Wawa and Witra Urania. Their offspring founded the gene pool for kennels such as: z Zeriby, spod Winnego Krzewu, z Henrykowa, Kawalkada, Reza, Moscic, ze Spiewogry, z Banciarni and Fervidus.

INT.PL.DK Ch Zupan z Kordegardy by Rumcajs z Jurty ex Lada z Kordegardy.

Ch Ustka z Kordegardy, World Winner'80 by Ch Doman z Kordegardy ex Dumka z Kordegardy. There are as many as 60 champions amongst Ustka's offspring.

Arabella's branch is very wide and active - more than 20 Polish Champions come from this branch.

Cedra spod Winnego Krzewu's bloodlines were developed from Arabella z Alty's branch. The most well-known dam coming from this line is Turnia z Szalasu Puchatkow, the foundation of 'z Banciarni' kennel and dam of 3 Polish champions. Another influencial dam coming from Bajda z Babiej Wsi's daughters are Beza z Lagiewnickiego Boru, dam of Miedza z Kordegardy (Belgium), Bomba z Kordegardy whose daughter Tama Delicja gave birth to 3 Polish Champions and Drumla z Kordegardy (1973), dam of the outstanding bitch, World Winner `83 Ch. Malwina z Kordegardy and granddam of another great bitch - World Winner `80 Ch. Ustka z Kordegardy.

Ch. Ustka z Kordegardy is dam of 3 excellent brood bitches: Polka z Kordegardy, Plaza z Kordegardy and Ch. Pajda z Kordegardy. Polka z Kordegardy through her daughter Garstka Sagittarius established 'z Wielgowa' kennel; Strozka Sagittarius established the 'Baltycka Rapsodia' kennel; Plaza z Kordegardy was

Turnia z Szalasu Puchatkow, the foundation bitch of 'z Banciarni' kennel.

Ch Duga-Jaga z Kordegardy by Ch Apasz z Bankowcow ex Plaza z Kordegardy and Ch Brussa z Doliny Biebrzy, by Apasz ex Majka z Kordegardy.

PL.CS Ch Jodla z Kordegardy by Ch Doman z Kordegardy
ex Lonka z Kordegardy.

the dam of Ch. Duga-Jaga z Kordegardy ('z Ameliowki' kennel), dam of 6 champions including Ch. Watra z Ameliowki ('Moscic' kennel) and Ch. Szczodra Arnika z Ameliowki ('z Jurajskiego Zrodla' kennel). Roza, a dam in z Wielgowa kennel, is Duga Jaga's granddaughter. Ch. Pajda z Kordegardy is grand dam of Ch. Brussa z Doliny Biebrzy and Brussa is dam of 6 champions in the kennel 'z Matecznika Diany'. Ch. Malwina z Kordegardy, mentioned earlier, is dam of World Winner `89 Ch. Arkonia z Kordegardy ('Skierdy' kennel) and Club Winner '87. The dams coming from her line who are important here are Club Winner '93 Ch. Maruna z Gangu Dlugich, dam of 6 champions and Zacierka z Gangu Dlugich, dam of 7 champions. Malwina's branch is not very wide but there were as many as 27 champions born.

Rzepicha z Psiego Raju was another bitch coming from Bajda z Babiej Wsi's daughters. Her daughter Ch. Domka z Psiego Raju ('z Nadwarcianskiej Doliny' kennel) gave birth to Ch. Agusia z Nadwarcianskiej Doliny ('z Ogrodka Magdy' kennel). Unfortunately this branch seems to be almost a dead branch and no longer active in the gene pool.

Kuma z Kordegardy, daughter of Diuna z Babiej Wsi, granddaughter of Bajda, was the dam of Ch. Garda Wtora z Kordegardy. Garda Wtora established the 'spod Zagla' kennel. In this branch there are Jodla z Kordegardy and Ch. Lada z Kordegardy as well.

Ch. Lada z Kordegardy is dam of Frytka z Kordegardy who founded 'Kontrapunkt' kennel. Lada's granddaughter, Ch. Chatka z Kordegardy, established 'Misiura' kennel. This branch also seems to be almost a dead branch.

Ch. Jodla z Kordegardy gave birth to Ch. Alegoria Agiponik ('ze Starego Lupkowa' kennel) whose daughter Duda ze Starego Lupkowa established the 'Akribeia' kennel and Gera ze Starego Lupkowa established the 'Agajax' kennel. Another daughter, Ajka Agiponik, continues through the 'z Armii Zbawienia' kennel.

The lines of Misia have developed very slowly and really just in the 1990s through the bitch Sawa Laka Stokrotek has it finally developed at the kennel 'Pony Klub'; Beta's line continues through the 'Rexer' kennel.

The last representative of Wiga's line was Domka-Bystra (1970). In this line there is Harfa z Kordegardy, dam of Amok Moniek. Harfa can be found in pedigrees of many Polish PONs.

Ania Dominiak's work on top producing sires and dams was compiled in September 2002 and will by its nature require annual updating and therefore some change in composition. The most important sires and dams identified are those whose great influence on the PON's development is expressed through the quantity and

Jemiola z Kordegardy by PL Ch Igor z Zeriby ex Plaza z Kordegardy, foundation bitch at 'Rawipon' kennel.

Ch Watra z Ameliowki, daughter of Duga-Jaga

quality of their progeny. It ranks the dogs based on the number of Polish champion and Junior champion offspring, but does not take in to account overseas progeny or overseas champions. It does however represent dogs both past and present. The number of champions is shown in brackets after the dog's name. The top producing dam is Zacierka z Gangu Dlugich (7) followed closely by PL Ch Brussa z Doliny Biebrzy, PL Ch Duga-Jaga z Kordegardy, Int.PL Ch Maruna z Gangu Dlugich, Ch. Chluba z Gangu Dlugich and Ch Miedza z Wielgowa, all with 6.

10. Looking to the Future

The Polski Owczarek Nizinny is now well established as both a show dog and companion dog. It is the responsibility of breeders to improve and maintain quality and to educate others, especially judges. The PON's construction is not complicated so there is no excuse for incompetent judging. Breeders and breed clubs must also educate on type - and the correct type - this may not necessarily be what is winning. It is essential to breed selectively and not to be content with mediocrity.

International cooperation between breeders, breed clubs and Kennel Clubs is the best way forward. It is Poland's responsibility to educate us all and our responsibility to listen and act accordingly.

I am sure that debates on size and tails will continue to rage within the breed, in some countries. Wouldn't it be simpler if we all worked to the same standard?

The PON has served as a working dog since the 16th century. We must preserve the breed, true to type, as the Polish people require - today and tomorrow.

I have made many friends throughout the world, all dedicated to improving the breed and frustrated by the interference of the few. Winning is not everything and no one is bigger than the breed. We should all feel privileged to be involved with such wonderful dogs.

The PON has survived many hardships, not least, two World Wars, and I am sure that it will continue to thrive now that it has so many devotees. It is our job to conserve it for the enjoyment of future generations.

References & Sources

Battaglia, C.L. *Breeding Better Dogs*, B.E.I. Publications, Atlanta, USA 1986.

Borkowski, T. *Present Understanding of the FCI Standard of the PON*, Miedzynarodowy Kongres Pona, Lodz, Poland, 2003.

Brace, A. *Essential Guide to Judging Dogs*, Ringpress Books, Herts, UK. 1994.

Braund, K. *The Uncommon Dog Breeds*, Arco, USA 1976.

Brown, E.J., Borkowski, T. & Supronowicz, M. *The Official Book of the Polish Lowland Sheepdog*, T.F.H. Publications Inc, NJ, USA, 1995.

Cole. R. *You be the Judge*, Dog News, USA, Dec 07, 2001.

Coppinger, R. Dogs - *A Startling New Understanding of Canine Origin, Behavior and Evolution*, University of Chicago Press, USA, 2002.

Dominiak, A. *Golden Jubilee of Polish Lowland Sheepdogs*, Miedzynarodowy Kongres Pona, Lodz, Poland, 2003.

Forelle, D. *About the Polish Lowland Sheepdog*, Pies Magazine, Poland 1975.

Jasica, L. *Judging the PON in the New Millennium*, Southern Polish Lowland Sheepdog Club (proposed), UK, 2002.

Kraemer, E.M. *The Polish Lowland Sheepdog - An Old, But A New Breed*

Larska, B. *Ksiega Championow 2000*, Zwiazek Kynologiczny w Polsce, Warsaw, Poland, 2000.

Larska, B. *Ksiega Miotow Polskich Owczarkow Nizinnych*, Wydawnictwo 'Tim', Olsztyn, Poland 1997.

Larska, B. *The Most Influential Mothers and Fathers, Passed Away*, Miedzynarodowy Kongres Pona, Lodz, Poland, 2003.

Lehtinen, H. & Lummelampi, C. *Where is Typical Movement Going*, www.toydogs.net/english/English.htm; extracts reproduced here by permission and copyrighted 1999 by its authors.

Padgett, G. *Prioritizing Genetic Defects*, www.newfdogclub.org

Page Elliott, R. *Dogsteps - A New Look*, Doral Publishing, Arizona, USQ, 2001.

Polish Kennel Club, *Polish Breeds*, Main Board of the Kennel Club in Poland, Warsaw, Poland, 2000.

Redlicki, M. *PON* Agencja Wydawnicza 'Ergos', Warsaw, Poland, 1996.

Szczepanski, W. *Morphological approach of PON's coat after initial laboratory tests*, Miedzynarodowy Kongres Pona, Lodz, Poland, 2003.

Various, *Pies Magazine* 1975, date and issue number unknown.

Various, *Polish Heritage*, Soft Vision Oficyna Wydawnicza, Szczecin, Poland, 2000.

Spira, H. *Canine Terminology*, Watermark Press, USA, 2002.

Willis, M. (interviewed by Packard, G.) *The Basic Toolkit for Responsible Breeders*, Institute for Genetic Disease Control, June 2001.

The translations from old Polish literature are approximate rather than literal. Breed registration details are taken from Ksiega Miotow Polskich Owczarkow Nizinnych.

Back cover picture: Ch.Int Ch. Antrosu Dobrany from Dorianblue, Group 2 at Mechelen, Belgium, 2003, judge Lucienne Jasica; photo by Karl Donvil.

ISBN 1-41204525-8